for Steve S.

Best wishes,
Burt Prelutsky

THE STORY OF MY LIFE

STARRING GROUCHO MARX * OSCAR LEVANT * BILLY WILDER * JACK WEBB * WILLIAM PETER BLATTY * LARRY GELBART * GEORGE C. SCOTT * GENE KELLY * GINGER ROGERS * NORMAN LLOYD * JACKIE GLEASON * STEPHEN CANNELL * GEORGE KENNEDY * MAE WEST * JACK ELAM * SUSAN STRASBERG * JACK BENNY * FRED ASTAIRE * SONNY TUFTS * SPIRO AGNEW * RICHARD DREYFUSS * ANDREA MARCOVICCI * VIC MORROW * JIMMY STEWART AND A CAST OF HUNDREDS!

by

BURT PRELUTSKY

BearManor
Media

Albany, Georgia

Published in the USA by
BearManor Media
P.O. Box 71426
Albany, GA 31708
www.BearManorMedia.com

Softcover Edition
ISBN-10: 1629331007
ISBN-13: 9781629331003

Printed in the United States of America

This book, like my life, is dedicated to my wife, Yvonne, who proves that the third time really is the charm.

MY LIFE & SOME OF MY TIMES

When I began writing this book my wife and friends would ask what I was working on. I would say it was my memoir, but I knew it wasn't going to be exactly that.

I would be writing about my life, but only those parts of it that involved notables with whom I had worked or whom I'd interviewed, and, in a few cases, befriended.

In short, I was writing a book that not only strangers might wish to read, but one I would even be interested enough to write.

It's not that my life has been boring. Far from it. But why should anyone who doesn't know me have the slightest interest in my parents or my two older brothers, or how I felt about them, or how I dealt with puberty or acne. I had read too many true life sagas, or at least started to read them where after the first hundred pages, the subject I was interested in reading about hadn't even been born yet.

Those people or their biographers may have thought it was essential that I knew all about their ancestors or the world into which they'd been born, but I begged to differ. If the ancestors had been that fascinating someone would have written a separate book about them.

Perhaps if you're someone like Mary, Queen of Scots, it's important to know about their parents and siblings, but not if you're Burt Prelutsky of Chicago and Los Angeles.

To me, the parts of my life that might be of some interest to other people are the parts where my life intersected the lives of people like Groucho Marx, Oscar Levant, George C. Scott, Jack Webb and William Peter Blatty.

And when you get right down to it, who'd know better?

Burt Prelutsky
North Hills, CA

TENNIS AND POKER, EVERYONE

I had played tennis fairly regularly from the time I was 13-years-old. At the time, I had a friend who played and offered to teach me. Early on, I could see there was a problem. He would show me how to hit the ball, but when we rallied, he wouldn't stroke it the way he told me. Instead, he would hit it underhand to make it easier for me to return his shot.

I told him I needed him to hit it correctly so I would see how he was doing it. In fact, I told him I would bet him 50 cents a set just so he would try. It worked. Within a few weeks I was beating him, so we were able to quit playing for money.

Over the years I had the privilege of playing tennis with a lot of people. Some, such as Billie Jean King and Bobby Riggs, I played so I could write about the experience. They were both better than me, but he was a nice guy and she was a sour puss.

The court that became my regular venue over the years was at the home of my friend, Merrill Heatter. Merrill was the nephew of radio's legendary Gabriel Heatter. He was also half of Heatter-Quigley, the extremely successful TV game show creators/producers. Their biggest success was *Hollywood Squares*, which combined a game show with comedy. And although it was such panelists as Paul Lynde, Wally Cox and Cliff Arquette (aka Charley Weaver) who got to deliver the jokes, most of them were written by Heatter. As I believe someone or other once said, anybody can be successful if they don't care who gets the credit. And if nobody said it, I'm more than happy to take the credit.

Because of Merrill's show biz connections, I got to play with Ray Anthony, Ross Martin, John Marley and Gussie Moran. But the most memorable occasion was when three of us were rallying, waiting for our fourth, who was Danny Welkes, a former agent at William Morris. He finally arrived accompanied by a tall guy with gray hair who looked

1

exactly like former Vice President Spiro Agnew. Turns out it was Spiro Agnew.

He looked better in tennis shorts than he looked on the court. There are few treats in the world that can match being teamed in doubles with a former V.P. and be able to say, "That one was yours, Spiro."

I wasn't prepared to like him, but when we all socialized after the game he showed us why he had been so successful as a politician. He was charming and funny, and if he hadn't been so corrupt and so dumb that he actually continued receiving bribes even after he was no longer the governor of Maryland, he could have wound up being president once Richard Nixon proved he was so corrupt and so dumb that he felt he had to cheat to win an election that was in the bag without breaking into the office of the DNC in the Watergate complex.

On other occasions, at the height of *Charley's Angels* popularity, I got to team up with Farrah Fawcett and play Dick and Pat Van Patten. She wasn't even as good as Spiro Agnew, but it wasn't as much fun saying, "That one was yours, Farrah."

I played tennis with George Peppard on his lawyer's court. The odd thing about playing tennis with a guy as big and as athletic-looking as Peppard is that he really wasn't very good.

A P.R. man once set up a tennis match with James Mason. The idea was we'd play a set and then do a lunch interview. I don't know if he couldn't run or if he just didn't like to run. At one point, he said that he preferred court tennis. I told him I had never heard of it, and he explained that one of the French kings had invented it. It seems what Mason liked about it was that you got to let the ball bounce two or three times before hitting it. I suppose that since a king invented it, the object was to hit the ball as close to your opponent as possible.

When we broke for lunch on the outdoor patio, I got to watch one of the strangest sights I had ever seen. Three older women were having lunch at a table, but apparently it was the table that club member Gilbert Roland clearly regarded as his personal property. There he stood, about five feet from the women, his arms folded across his chest, glaring at them. They finally caved in and asked the waiter to move them to a different table.

I never got to play tennis with Robert Duvall, whom I'd heard was one of the best of the Hollywood crowd. Of those I did get to play with and against, the best were Dick Van Patten and his son, Vince, who actually turned pro for a while.

To look at the Van Pattens, which included Dick's wife and their other two sons, you would take them to be one of those blond, good-looking, wholesome families you see in TV commercials selling toothpaste, winter sports equipment, or SUVs.

But the fact is that when Dick wasn't playing tennis or in front of the cameras he was at the racetrack. As for Vince, the first time I encountered him he was seated across the table from me at a poker game. He was 16 at the time. I discovered that he loved gambling so much he had a disguise, that included a wig, a beard, and a grungy old baseball cap, packed away in his car so that he could sneak into poker casinos and play in Gardena (a suburb where poker was legal, but 16-year-old players weren't).

As for Dick, he loved the ponies so much that if he wasn't working and it was the off-season at local tracks Santa Anita and Hollywood Park, he would fly up to San Francisco from Van Nuys so he could bet the horses at Bay Meadows. After the track closed for the day, he would fly home and go off to one of his four or five weekly poker games.

A few years later I was living in Carmel, 350 miles north of L.A., while engaged in a custody battle for my son. One day, while at the downtown courthouse pleading my case, I ran into Vinnie. I asked him what he was doing in court and he explained that he had recently turned 21 and discovered that his former business manager had embezzled a lot of the money he had made as a kid actor. He was suing to recover what he could.

I asked him what else he was up to. "Playing poker, of course."

I asked him how he was doing. "I did pretty well last night."

"Big game?"

"Pretty big."

Now if I said "Pretty big," it might mean that a few hundred dollars had been won or lost. But when a Van Patten says it, my ears perk up.

"How big?" I asked.

"Well, $95,000 changed hands."

"That's pretty big," I gulped.

Until then the biggest game I knew about was one I hadn't played in. The reason I wasn't there was because I knew that Gabe Kaplan would be. I had already played with him, and it hadn't been any fun, even though I came out winners.

The following week the buy-in was raised to $5,000. That didn't mean you had to risk it all. You were allowed to put as many chips as you liked in your pockets, leaving only what you were prepared to risk on the table. But if someone raised you, you couldn't suddenly pull additional chips out of your pocket. You were limited to only the original pot. If there were two other players betting they would have a separate pot, and if one of them had the best hand he would scoop both pots. If you won you would only get the original pot; the winner between the two of them would take the second pot.

As it was told to me, two players opted to keep all $5,000 on the table. As luck would have it, they were the two who went head-to-head in the first hand of the night. They were Gabe Kaplan and an insurance executive.

Kaplan, thanks to all the money that was pouring into his coffers as the result of being the star and the creator of the hit sitcom *Welcome Back, Kotter*, loved to bluff. In fact, the vibes I got from having played against him was that he didn't really enjoy winning a pot if he actually had the best hand.

So on the first hand of the evening he ran a bluff and the insurance man had a flush and took the pot. Kaplan, pointing out that the other guy now had $10,000, asked if he could buy in for $10,000. It was allowed. On the next hand the two of them once again went head-to-head. This time, Kaplan had a straight but the insurance man had another flush.

For some reason, even though the insurance man now had $20,000, Kaplan only asked to buy $10,000. It was a wise move because, as the fates would have it, he once again went mano-a-mano with the insurance man. And although Kaplan had a full house, the other fellow's was bigger.

So, in something like 10 minutes, Gabe Kaplan lost $25,000 he would not be able to deduct on his income taxes and the insurance man won $25,000 that the IRS would never know about.

One regular poker game that went on for years took place every Tuesday night in the Studio City condo of actor Ned Wertimer, who played the white doorman on *The Jeffersons*.

Some of the regulars were Roger Price, Jack Elam, Don Galloway, Alex Rocco, David Huddleston and Ronny Cox. Once in a while, Lee Majors would play. But, Majors actually preferred fighting. So, on occasion, he would leave the game early and go across the street to a bar. More than once, we would look out the window and see him in the bar's parking lot duking it out with some other drunk. We never knew who started it, but the way he played poker, he was probably saving money by fighting with strangers when he would otherwise be losing to friends.

Ronny Cox, a very good actor most people might remember best as the villain in RoboCop, was a very good poker player. He might have been the very best I ever played against, except for one fatal flaw. There were many times when we'd be playing seven-card stud - a game in which if you stick it out to the end, you wind up with seven cards in front of you, four of them exposed, three of them face down - and Ronny would look at the remaining players. Then one by one, he would call out your hands as if they were all face up.

He would say, "Burt has a busted flush, Roger has two small pair and Dick has aces." Then he would sit for another couple of seconds and then toss away three of a kind, saying something like "No, Roger made his full house."

More often than not, Ronny had been right the first time, but had talked himself out of it.

Now I can't vouch for what cards everyone else was holding, but he was always right about my hand. It was almost like a magic act, except it was a magic act in which instead of the magician getting loose from the chains, he would wind up handcuffing himself.

I CAN'T DANCE, DON'T MAKE ME

Two of the people I most wanted to interview because I had been a fan seemingly my entire life were Gene Kelly and Ginger Rogers. I could hardly believe my good fortune when I had the opportunity on back to back days, Kelly in his longtime home in Beverly Hills, Rogers at her home in the desert.

When it came to comparing Kelly to Astaire, I tended to give the edge to Astaire. Not because I necessarily preferred his style and grace to Kelly's strength and athleticism, but because I preferred the songs in Astaire's movies. Whereas Astaire had the likes of Irving Berlin, Cole Porter, Johnny Mercer, Harold Arlen, Jerome Kern, and the Gershwins writing songs specifically for him, Kelly was often cast in period musicals, singing and dancing to tunes that were already 30 or 40 years old by the time he got around to them.

There were a few exceptions, such as Kern's immortal "Long Ago and Far Away" in *Cover Girl*. But for the most part, Kelly's best music had come to him second-hand in the form of "An American in Paris," "Broadway Melody," "Slaughter on 10th Avenue," and the various Arthur Freed/Nacio Herb Brown ditties in *Singin' in the Rain*.

Another problem I had with Kelly's movies is that within minutes of the finish line, he would suddenly stop everything in order to devote 15 or 20 minutes to a lengthy production number, such as the ballet in *An American in Paris* or "Broadway Melody" in *Singin' in the Rain*. It wasn't that they weren't well done, but coming, as they did, in the homestretch made them seem like clumsy additions and managed to make both movies feel as if they were an hour longer than they were.

But it was hard to resist Kelly's charm, with his slightly lopsided grin and his inimitable singing voice. The shock came when the door to his home was opened by his wife, and I discovered it was because Kelly could barely walk across the room. To find him in that condition was as sad as meeting a favorite ballplayer from your youth and finding that

7

you were now in better shape than he is and that you could probably now beat him at his own game.

The truth is, that after coming home from one of his movies when I was nine or ten years old and realizing that there in our living room was a low chair with a padded seat and back, I couldn't wait for my folks and my two older brothers to be out of the house so I could use it as a prop. The moment that opportunity presented itself I jumped up on the seat with one foot while placing my other foot against the back. I then rode the chair backwards so it landed with a soft thud and I skipped off. So far as I was concerned, I was Gene Kelly.

It has since occurred to me that I had leapt to the same conclusion that I'm sure generations of young Americans had come to, which was that if he could do it, we could, too. It never occurred to me or any other sane person that we could mimic Fred Astaire. After all, you had to get all dressed up and have a partner to carry that off, and there are precious few homes that have white tie and tails, or Ginger Rogers, for that matter, hanging in the closet.

Frankly, it's a wonder that any former movie dancer can still walk around in his 60s. It's not the dancing or the rehearsing, exactly, that cripples most of them to some extent, it's the fact that those gorgeous shiny floors you see them dancing across aren't made of wood, they're made of cement. Actors only say they suffer for their art; dancers actually do.

Gene Kelly was as charming and likeable in person as he was on screen, but I still left his home feeling, as I often have, that life isn't fair. If there was ever anyone who shouldn't have to limp slowly across the carpet to see someone out of his house, it's Gene Kelly.

But at least he could still walk, even if not terribly well.

The next day I drove out to Rancho Mirage to interview Ginger Rogers. When I passed through the gate she was sitting outside on her patio by the pool. As I got closer, I discovered she was seated in a wheelchair.

She had certainly put on a lot of weight since the last time I'd seen her on screen. At this point I should probably confess that I not only thought she was a great dancer, (as someone once observed, she not only did everything that Fred Astaire did, but she did it backward and in heels), but I thought she was a great comedienne. Although she got her Oscar for the schmaltzy *Kitty Foyle*, I would have given it to her for *Bachelor Mother* or *The Major & the Minor*.

As it turned out, she was so frisky and high-spirited that it was much easier to overlook her physical limitations than it had been a day earlier with Gene Kelly. At one point, it being a warm day, she suggested we have lemonade. I offered to go inside to tell her assistant. But she gestured for me to remain seated. Instead, she put two fingers in her mouth and gave such a loud whistle, I thought it just possible that a New York taxi might pull up at the curb. It certainly got her assistant's attention.

One thing I had noticed about her in the Astaire movies was the way she listened. I mean when he was singing to her. Over the years, I had seen a lot of people, both men and women, being sung to on screen, but about the most they ever did was smile, as if biding their time until it was time for them to show us what singing was all about. But when Astaire sings, Rogers actually reacts to the lyrics as if he were speaking, not singing. When I paid her the compliment, she said, "Yes, it's called acting."

When we went inside, she proudly showed me a drawing hanging on the wall. It was a drawing of himself that George Gershwin had given her. I don't recall the inscription exactly, but I got the definite impression that he had done more than write a few songs for her.

She admitted nothing, but she did say that after five marriages and five divorces, her only real matrimonial regret was that she didn't stay married to number two in the series, Lew Ayres.

A few months later I arranged to meet and interview one more dancer. It was Tommy Rall. He wasn't as famous as the others, but I think that had something to do with the fact that by the time he came to Hollywood, musicals were pretty much on the way out. But if you ever saw him on screen, I suspect you would remember him. He was, along with Bob Fosse and Bobby Van, one of the three harlequins

9

who danced with Ann Miller in *Kiss Me, Kate*. In *My Sister Eileen*, he performed the exhilarating competition dance in the alley behind the burlesque theater with Bob Fosse. His finest moment, though, came in *7 Brides for 7 Brothers*, in which he was the brother in the red shirt.

As I waited for him to show up at the Jewish deli in Santa Monica, I suddenly realized he didn't know what I looked like, and I had no idea what he looked like 40 or so years after I'd last seen him dancing on screen. Every time some old guy came through the door I stared to see if I could spot the young Rall lurking in there somewhere. Unfortunately, in a Jewish deli, almost every guy, including me, looks as if he's spent several long years dancing on cement.

When Rall finally entered I spotted him immediately. He just looked like an older version of the guy I remembered. No limping, no crutches, no wheelchair. Perhaps he'd been lucky coming to the movies so late in the game.

The thing I recall best was that when I reported that in response to my asking him who he thought the best dancer he'd ever known was, Gene Kelly, without hesitation, said "Tommy Rall," Rall didn't seem to think it was such a big deal. For the life of me, I don't know if Rall didn't think very much of Gene Kelly or if he assumed that had to be Kelly's answer since it was so obviously true. The fact is that when I had asked Kelly the question, the answer in my own head had been Tommy Rall, and I had been flabbergasted that someone as knowledgeable as Kelly had confirmed my opinion.

Actually, what Kelly had said was that Tommy Rall wasn't the best at any single dance style, but that when you took every style, including tap, swing, and ballet into consideration, nobody could touch him.

DIPPING A TOE
INTO SHARK-INFESTED WATERS

When I entered UCLA, it was with the notion that by the time I got out, I would be well on my way to being a novelist or at least a short story writer. As it happens, I was writing professionally, but as, of all things, a movie reviewer.

I had gotten tired of attending school with so many of the same people since the second grade, so I decided to attend UC Santa Barbara instead of UCLA. But after a single semester, I concluded that I liked them better than the ones I hadn't gone to school with for the past decade, and transferred down to UCLA. Besides, UCLA was the size of a small city, so I could pretty easily avoid anyone I wished to avoid.

What had happened during that semester was that a high school friend had started reviewing TV for the *Daily Bruin*, and when asked if he knew any writers who could write as well as he could, he mentioned me. After meeting with the editor I told him I wasn't interested in being a reporter, but I would like a crack at writing a humor column.

Unfortunately, having just turned 18, I wasn't sure what to write about, humorously or otherwise. What I came up with was a somewhat surrealistic approach that consisted of coming up with a pun that would conclude the piece and then backing up about 500 words in order to lead up to the hilarious payoff. Well, maybe not hilarious, but funnier than anything else appearing in the *Bruin*.

The problem, I soon discovered, was that the guys at the printing shop didn't get puns, and would "correct" them. I was told to include "stet" on the page to warn them not to change my copy. But I was afraid that the "stet" would wind up in the article. So, for the rest of the semester, I would show up at the printer and hang around until midnight to protect the copy from their well-intentioned efforts to clean up my mistakes.

Fortunately, by the time the next semester rolled around, the student who had been reviewing movies for the *Bruin* had graduated and his job was up for grabs. The two competitors were myself and a young female student. We were both supposed to attend a screening that night at the Director's Guild theater. There were supposed to be passes for both of us, but when I arrived, I couldn't get in. Either Shirley Mae Fullmer had brought a date and didn't realize that he was therefore the recipient of the second pass or she intentionally sabotaged me. But I later got to know Shirley and was able to conclude that it had been an honest mistake, either on her part or by the guy at the door.

Although I couldn't get in to see the movie, the guy at the door did allow me to take a one-page flyer that included the title, *Seven Hills of Rome*, and the star, Mario Lanza.

Having seen a few Lanza musicals by then, I was confident that I could carry it off. After all, I knew the tenor billed as the successor to Caruso would sing an assortment of pop tunes and operatic arias and would, after a hitch or two, get the girl. So while Shirley was dutifully sitting through it and taking notes, I was home banging out my review.

I got the gig and, as a consolation prize of sorts, she got to be the editor of the *Daily Bruin*.

By this time, they had initiated a weekly insert called Intro. Its four pages would include reviews of movies, plays, books and TV.

Getting to be the movie reviewer was great, except that now I had to actually watch the movies. But at least now I had something to actually write about, and, more often than not, Hollywood would see to it that I would have plenty of targets for ridicule.

I not only continued to review movies for a few years, but during my second year on the job, a recent start-up, *Los Angeles Magazine*, hired me to review for them. It was my first professional gig, but only barely. I was being paid one-half cent a word, and because I wasn't bothering to count them, I naturally assumed there was someone in the office who was being paid more to count my words than I was to write them.

In my final year of writing for the *Bruin*, there was an expanded

Christmas edition of Intro. So, instead of my usual review of just one or two movies and placement on page two, there were four movies. Although I actually liked the two movies I reviewed on the second page, the other two were major releases, *Exodus* and *Pepe*, and the editor had chosen to plaster them across the front page of the insert.

I hated both movies, partly though not entirely because the former ran or rather creaked along for nearly three and a half hours and *Pepe*, which lasted exactly three hours but seemed longer, was George Sidney's attempt to repeat Mike Todd's success with *Around the World in 80 Days*. Unfortunately, where Todd had Cantinflas, David Niven, and Shirley MacLaine in the leads and an Oscar-winning script that included S.J. Perelman in the writing credits and Victor Young's Oscar-winning song and score, *Pepe* had Cantinflas, Dan Dailey, and Shirley Jones, and a script and score that could have been the work of Sidney's brother-in-law, so long as he possessed neither writing nor musical talent.

In any case, Sidney took umbrage and threatened, as head of the Director's Guild of America, to cut off grants and scholarships to UCLA. The Director of Publications at UCLA, an adult, begged for a meeting to iron out these differences. A few days later he and my editor were invited to the DGA to discuss the situation. I was cordially invited to stay home.

Apparently, Mr. Sidney said he didn't care what I had to say about *Pepe*, which was pretty much what every other critic had said about the snoozearama. But, he went on to say, "I have always felt very close to UCLA and it would pain me to cut off the scholarships, but anyone who didn't like *Exodus* is obviously an anti-Semite."

When my editor pointed out that I was in fact Jewish, Sidney's response was: "They're the worst kind!"

The head of Publications managed to work out a compromise with Sidney, which resulted in UCLA continuing to enjoy the largesse from the Director's Guild. Because I had recently dropped out of college, while continuing to hone my craft on the Bruin, the compromise consisted of running a little disclaimer at the end of my reviews for the remainder of the semester. It read: "Burt Prelutsky, a former student, is no longer affiliated with UCLA."

In short, my stupid opinions were strictly my own, just as they'd always been. I just wish I could have reviewed *Pepe* and *Exodus* the same way I'd reviewed *7 Hills of Rome*, by staying home, thus saving myself nearly seven hours of agony.

One of the reasons I had dropped out of school was because the two writing classes I took were a total waste of time. In the first case, the professor had assigned us to write a 500-word piece. No problem. However, when he passed them back to us, mine was ungraded. I asked him why that was. He said he didn't consider humor to be writing.

When he was collecting our next assignment he asked me if it was humorous. I told him I hoped so. He handed it back, confirming that it hadn't been a bout of temporary insanity when he'd rejected the first assignment. He left me no choice but to get up and leave the classroom, never again to lighten his doorway or his reading material.

My next writing professor had apparently only sold two magazine articles in his life. I never got to read them, but he had sold them to the male adventure magazines that were still popular in those days, magazines like Argosy and Stag that seemed to appreciate stories by men who loved to venture into the wilderness and then come out to write about how they'd been held as sex slaves by African pygmies or lusty busty women who lived along the Amazon.

I never quite got the knack of writing that sort of thing, although I did decide that, all else being equal, I would prefer to risk my life in the jungles of the Amazon.

But, looking back, I believe I got more out of my college years than many of my fellow students. It's true that I never did get a degree, but that may have been a blessing because it prevented me from ever falling back on teaching when things would periodically run dry in my career.

UCLA gave me plenty of opportunity to write, and I took advantage of it by writing constantly for not only the *Daily Bruin*, but for the campus literary magazine and for *Satyr*, the humor magazine, whose pages also included the work of young Harry Shearer, Joel Siegel, and Hank Hinton.

Although I would never have occasion to meet George Sidney, the experience at UCLA, where he had to settle on bullying a college publication because he couldn't get away with threatening the movie critics at the *New York Times*, *Time* magazine or the *L.A. Times*, guys who had also panned *Pepe*, did help to prepare me for the sort of self-serving hypocrisy and bullshit I would often encounter once I began working in Hollywood.

DOES THE PIG HAVE ANY LINES?

When I left UCLA, I had no idea what I was going to do with my life. Fortunately, Geoff Miller, my editor at *Los Angeles* magazine, where I was still being paid half a cent-a-word for my movie reviews, was dating a woman who worked at an advertising agency. He suggested I try to get a job at Carson/Roberts.

All I knew about advertising was what I had glommed from movies like *The Hucksters*, which meant I knew that three martini lunches were the norm and that creative people had to sublimate their talents in order to peddle toothpaste and potato chips. I figured I could handle it.

What I didn't know at the time was who did what at agencies or what their titles were. As I recall, I addressed my query letter to something called an office manager. Luckily, the letter wound up in the hands of the creative director, a funny guy named Ken Sullet. He, in turn, thought my letter was funny. Perhaps it was the line about my needing a job because my mother wanted me out of the house.

I found that I liked copywriting even though very little of my work ever got produced. But, inasmuch as I was a junior copywriter, I didn't get many shots to spread my wings, assuming I had any wings. In my lowly role, I was usually given the scut assignments on our biggest account, which happened to be Mattel Toys.

One of the really mind-numbing chores I was handed was to write the little blurbs in the Mattel catalogue describing Barbie's outfits. I wracked my brain and my Thesaurus to find adjectives to best describe taffeta.

As bad as that was, even worse were writing commercials for Mattel's various talking dolls. I set out to write a spot in which a child would appear to carry on a conversation with Chatty Cathy. But I was told that was a no-no. Somebody, I suppose it was the FCC, had a rule that we couldn't show a doll doing something it couldn't do. And as the dolls all worked off a string-pull that would have them delivering random lines, there was no way for a little girl to actually have a conversation, unless it went something like this: Girl: "Would you like a bath?" Doll: "Mama." Girl: "I said would you like a bath?" Doll: "Cathy hungry." Girl: "You're beginning to really piss me off. Now do you want a bath or don't you?"

A commercial in which a little girl vents her frustration by yanking off a doll's head might win a prize at some Polish film festival, but it wasn't what Mattel was looking for.

What made the assignment particularly frustrating was that I did need to incorporate as many of the doll's lines as I could in the commercial, even if I couldn't pretend it could carry on a conversation that would be reminiscent of Oscar Wilde and George Bernard Shaw at their wittiest, but Mattel didn't have a list of Cathy's lines. But they were pretty sure there were 22 of them.

So I set out to find out the extent of her vocabulary. After pulling her string for about 20 minutes, I believe I had jotted down 10 of them. Unfortunately, I shared an office that was divided into three cubicles with walls that only went up about five feet, falling about two feet shy of the ceiling. Finally, my fellow juniors gave up and pleaded for mercy. The only place I could find where I wouldn't drive anyone but myself crazy was on the stairwell between the second and third floors.

I never did reach the magic number, even after an hour of string-pulling.

It wasn't all in vain, though. When I visited my brother and his family, I discovered that I knew way more about Barbie, Ken and Cathy, than my seven-year-old niece.

The physical set-up of our little office was the cause of one of my more embarrassing moments. One morning, while seated at my desk, I heard my two office-mates, Jill Murray and Peyton Bailey, whispering and giggling like school girls.

Because, as I said, our partitions didn't reach the ceiling, you could always hear what the others were saying. What I managed to overhear was enough to convince me that our ad agency was a hot bed of, well, hot beds. If what the ladies were saying was true, everyone in the place, aside from me, was having a torrid affair. It's a wonder that any work got done.

Being new to the job, I hardly knew anyone's name, but I was certainly curious to find out who these people were. I gathered that Constance and Allison Mackenzie, Rodney Harrington and Betty Anderson, were the principal players in this immorality play that was taking place all around me.

Finally, my curiosity got the best of me and I let the ladies know I had heard their gossip, and now I wanted to know who these people were and in which departments they worked.

They shared a good laugh at my expense, and then explained that they were merely rehashing the previous evening's episode of *Peyton Place*.

That was their story, anyway, and they were sticking to it.

One thing I was proud of was that I made a point of trying to find out how much money other people were being paid, and sometimes I succeeded.

Proving that I could play the hero as well as the fool, I managed to discover that a copywriter named Bob who was one step up from my status, and a real pain in the posterior, was making $12,000-a-year. Not terrible back in those days for a guy in his mid-20s, especially not one who would have obviously stabbed everyone he knew in the back for an office on the third floor.

I then learned that a woman who was roughly his age and who worked on roughly the same level of accounts was only being paid $8,000. I walked into her office, sat down, and asked her if she knew what the schmuck in the next office -- Bob -- was making. She said she didn't and then pretended she didn't care to know. So I told her.

If she was shocked to learn he was making 50% more than her, she didn't show it. I pointed out she had just as much experience and worked on accounts that billed as much as his. I told her that

19

the bosses were getting away with -- if not murder, certainly with underpaying her -- and that she should ask for a raise.

She said she wouldn't dare. She said if they thought she deserved more money, they would have paid her more. She was driving me crazier than Chatty Cathy had.

I explained that the world didn't work that way.

I told her she was behaving as if the question wasn't whether they would pay her more or if they wouldn't, but whether they would pay her more or fire her.

I said that if they had wanted to fire her, she would have been gone long before this. Finally, I told her I was absolutely certain that she would go upstairs that very day and ask for her raise. When she asked me how I could be so sure, I said: "Because if you don't, I'm going to keep coming in here every day and remind you that Bob is being paid 50% more than you are."

The way I said "Bob," it was perfectly clear that we both knew that Bob was an obnoxious idiot, and how shameful it was to be paid less than he was.

Naturally, it worked. She went upstairs and, sure enough, they fired her.

You folks are so easy. Of course they didn't fire her. She got her raise. Ask yourselves: would I have related this story if I had gotten the poor girl fired?

But it was I who soon discovered a very odd thing about the world of advertising. Even though my talents had been wasted writing drivel about Barbie's wardrobe, it was enough that I was a copywriter at Carson/Roberts. One day, my phone rang. It was the creative director at Doyle/Dane/Bernbach.

Would I possibly be interested in working at D/D/B? Would I! Not only did the agency have the reputation of being the most creative shop in the business, but they would double my salary and, best of all, it was even closer to my apartment than Carson/Roberts.

So off I went. Although I only spent two years in advertising, a year at both places, I would say that the folks I worked with were easily the brightest groups I have ever encountered. They tended to be funny, irreverent, and they drank a lot.

Next to the people, the thing I liked best about advertising was, oddly enough, the tight deadlines. I am by nature a very impatient fellow. I like movies that wrap up in under two hours, novels that don't overstay their welcome by running on much past 350 pages, and writing assignments that need to be completed in a hurry so a person can move on to solving the next problem.

The only drawback was that I was still regarded as a junior copywriter, so the plum assignments went elsewhere. While my colleagues were working with the likes of Sandy Duncan, Rodney Allen Rippy, and Orson Welles, on award-winning commercials, I was stuck writing for a pig. No joke.

One of the trademarks of the work turned out by D/D/B was that they refused to merely be clever in their ads, commercials, and billboards. Bill Bernbach insisted that the client provide the agency with something upon which to hang a campaign. There had to be a product difference. I recall that held true even when the agency signed a salt company. I mean salt is just salt, after all. But Bernbach had insisted on having a new and improved salt container designed and manufactured before he'd accept them as a client.

Well, one day my assignment was to come up with a campaign for a brand of bread sold in the upper northwest. The product difference, I learned, was that our chief competitor's brand was made with lard. Our bread was made with something else. I don't remember what, but it was enough of a difference for me.

My brainstorm was to illustrate how awful lard was by showing its source, the biggest, ugliest pig they could find. The commercial opened with the pig staring straight at the camera while an off-screen voice said: "This is lard."

I thought it was great, although I was taken aback when the director asked me if the pig had any lines. The question had caught me so far off-balance that for a minute I wondered if I had heard right.

Then I realized this was TV. The pig could have put on a straw hat, picked up a cane and gone into a buck-and-wing, if I had wanted.

Instead, I told the director that the pig had no lines this time. But if the commercial had the impact I imagined it would, the pig might very well be starring in his own sitcom next season.

Well, I was right about the impact, though not quite the way I had expected.

I didn't get to see it premier on TV because the market for the bread was limited to Washington. But I did get the news the next day that the commercial had run at dinnertime, and the local station had been flooded with irate callers, insisting that the sight of the pig had been so disgusting they couldn't eat.

The commercial never ran again.

I didn't feel so bad for myself, but I really felt the pig could have had a big future in the business.

The one time I felt I had really hit my stride was when I was handed the Crown Russe print campaign. Crown Russe was a mid-priced vodka. I came up with what I thought were two excellent notions. The first was an ad that proclaimed that if you were paying more than, say, $3.49 for a fifth or whatever Crown Russe sold for, you were paying for the label. That was a slam at Kamchatka, which was the number one seller at the time and went for something like $4.29.

My other idea was a series of print ads that would show a picture of a Bloody Mary, a screwdriver, or a greyhound, with the caption: How to Get the Big Kids to Drink Their Juice. The copy would point out all the healthy benefits provided by tomato juice, orange juice, and grapefruit juice, never mentioning that along with all the vitamins they'd be ingesting, two or three of them would have you under the table.

But as luck would have it, my genius went unrecognized when the head copywriter preferred his own idea, which was to point out that "Crown Russe" rhymed with "juice."

Looking back, the two years weren't a total waste. I did get the nice lady at Carson/Roberts her raise.

NOT EXACTLY A HILLBILLY

I recall seeing Roger Price on TV variety shows in the early 50s. His act consisted of holding a drawing pad and sketching odd-looking pictures. When completed, he would gaze into the camera and deliver a gag caption.

One of them that became quite famous was of a straight line that cut the page in half. On the left side, you saw a small black triangle above the line; on the right side of the page, was a much larger triangle. The caption was: "A ship arriving too late to save a drowning witch."

I understood it was clever, but I not only didn't laugh, I couldn't even bring myself to smile. That was because the man with the sketch pad wore horn-rimmed glasses, had a nasty-looking mustache, and a glower that seemed to dare you to make a sound, let alone laugh at what he seemed to regard as very serious business.

Although I became aware with the passage of time that Roger Price was a satirist best-known for a series of humorous books called *Mad Libs*, which lent itself to a party game in which various people would suggest adverbs and nouns to fill in blanks in a written narrative. The results would then be read out, with results that were sometimes hilarious, sometimes just surrealistic.

He also had another series of books devoted to drawings like the drowning witch that were titled *Droodles*. He also had a book titled *What Not to Name the Baby*, which gave funny meanings to certain names, warning parents that attaching such a name to a newborn would doom it to a life of debauchery or worse.

As an adult, I was finally able to acknowledge that Price had a sense of humor, but I was still troubled by the sight of him on our old Philco TV. Although he had a West Virginia twang, he had the look of a New England Puritan who would brook no nonsense, and would have locked you in a stock as soon as look at you. He looked like he would have considered Cotton Mather a little too frivolous for his taste, as being more likely to rescue a drowning witch than to burn one.

I hadn't given Price much thought until one day when a female writer named Marcia invited me to tag along one Sunday when she paid Larry Sloan a visit at his beach house in Malibu. Although the plan had been to spend the entire afternoon, shortly after we arrived, Sloan happened to mention that he had heard from his partner in the publishing house, Roger Price, who was visiting from New York and said he might be stopping by.

The blood appeared to drain from Marcia's face. Now, understand, Marcia was no shrinking violet. She was built something like a small tank. You don't expect small tank people to look frightened simply because another writer might be dropping in for a visit.

When I asked Marcia what the problem was, I wasn't too surprised when she said she had known Roger when she lived in New York and that he was the meanest man she had ever known.

I'm not sure how long we stuck around, but I was aware that every time we would hear a car slow down on Pacific Coast Highway, she would go silent and strike a pose that resembled a hunting dog going on point. I'm sure I was doing the same, and was greatly relieved when she made her excuses to Larry and we made our getaway.

The next time that Roger's name cropped up, I was interviewing some guy who had written a book for Price/Stern/Sloan at a restaurant on La Cienega Blvd. When it was over the P/S/S publicist suggested I accompany her to their headquarters a block away. She said she was sure that Larry Sloan would be delighted to see me and wish to thank me for doing the interview.

I assured her that thanks weren't necessary, but I walked her back. When we got there, Larry said hello and told me that Roger Price was lying down in the back room and would love to meet me. I tried to beg off, insisting that I was already late for another appointment and begging him not to wake up Price, that meeting me was no big deal.

I don't know what I expected, but whatever it was, it's not what I got. If ever a human being had ever resembled one of those dogs that loped, all legs and floppy ears, through a thousand cartoons, it was Roger. You got everything but the tongue hanging out of the side of his mouth.

He not only couldn't have been nicer and more complimentary about my work, but he was asking me where I lived and when I told him, asked about housing prices in the area because he was thinking of moving out.

Whatever I said must have clinched the deal because within weeks, he was living on a hill in Studio City, two miles from my house.

Frankly, I couldn't see why Marcia had been so frightened. Where women were concerned, Roger had the manners of an old southern colonel. Or so it seemed. It turned out that he was downright courtly when it came to the women who were married or involved with his friends.

All other women were fair game, even if Roger didn't always play fair. One night, for example, my wife and I were joining Roger and his date, who turned out to be a very attractive Jewish accountant.

As luck would have it, we arrived at the restaurant at the same time.

As I held the door open for my wife and Roger's date, I felt a hand grasp my shoulder from behind. When I turned, Roger, who was quite tall, was leaning in and whispering into my ear: "I'm Doctor Pincus."

Okay, I got it. Tonight he was a Jewish physician. I don't know at what point his date would figure out that my friend was neither Jewish nor a doctor, but I suspected that she would catch on no later than the hors d'oeuvres that someone who had a West Virginia twang, was a partner in a publishing house, couldn't name the High Holidays, and had written for Bob Hope, probably wasn't Jewish and didn't have a medical practice on the side.

But this was Hollywood, so she probably wasn't even an accountant.

As I said, Roger could be the epitome of gallantry when it came to women who were clearly off limits, but when it came to those who were available, but apparently not to him, he could be outrageous.

On another occasion, we were once again double-dating with

25

Roger. This time, the lady was the ex-wife of a comedy writer. The plan was for us to pick the two of them up at her community property home in Beverly Hills. Unfortunately, someone decided we should dine at a Chinese restaurant that was nearly in the next county.

We got through dinner in fine fashion, but then, while waiting for the check to arrive, Roger and his date had a whispering conversation. I can only assume he was inviting himself to stay over at her place, and she was putting the kibosh on the idea. At any rate, the next thing I knew, Roger punched her in the arm. I feared he had broken it, but apparently that wasn't the case because she merely glowered at him.

Nobody said a word. We paid the check and left, and still nobody uttered a word.

In fact, during the hour or so it took me to drive back to the woman's house, my wife at my side, Roger and his victim sitting on opposite ends of the back seat, nobody said a single word. It was an hour, but the drive seemed to last a month.

When I dropped them off, nobody even said good-bye.

Driving off, I said to my wife, "Well, that seemed to go well. Can't wait to do it again."

In my life, I have known a large number of oddballs, but Roger may have been the oddest. For one thing, he had sophisticated tastes in literature and the arts. Even at an advanced age, he decided to start taking up the piano after not having played in decades. Mainly, it was because he wanted to be able to play the subtle piano works of Eric Satie.

He was much more of a football fan than I was, and somehow coaxed me into joining him in betting on pro football games with a Chinese restaurant owner in the San Fernando Valley who doubled as a bookie. The problem was that, like all bookies, he made his profit on the vig, short for vigorish, which means that when you lost $100, you had to pay him $100, but when you won $100, you only collected $90.

For the bookie, the other advantage was that whether we won or lost, we would wind up paying for our Chinese lunch. I finally convinced Roger we should simply bet against each other. We saved on the vigorish, but we missed out on the curry shrimp and egg rolls.

Years after visiting Larry Sloan's beach house with Marcia, Roger invited me to tag along on a visit. This time, Larry was working with a writer, Bob Einstein, a comedian who was better known as his alter ego, a daredevil he called Super Dave Osborne. In other quarters, he was known as a son of the old radio comic known as Parkyakarkus and as the older brother of writer-director Albert Brooks.

As they were in the last stages of designing Einstein's book, Sloan suggested that Roger and I take a walk on the beach with Einstein's date. As the three of us strolled in the sunshine, the young woman who was very blonde, buxom, and short, told us she had been a gymnast in high school up in Oregon, but was eager to get into show business. When we asked her if she'd found any work, she said she had been in a movie and also done a TV pilot. Except that she had actually received two pay checks, which put her two up on most girls from Oregon who come to Hollywood hoping to be, say, the next Sally Struthers, this one was Sally Struthers.

Within a couple of months, she was appearing on screen in *Five Easy Pieces* with Jack Nicolson and Karen Black, and appearing on TV's *All in the Family* as Archie Bunker's daughter, Gloria Stivic.

Go figure.

Although Roger didn't deal well with sexual frustration, he rarely seemed to experience it. He always or nearly always seemed to have women around, going places with him and even co-hosting his parties. I don't know if they had expectations of being the fifth Mrs. Price, but it was never meant to be.

I only knew one of his four ex-wives, the Jewish one who had been the mother of his son and daughter. Among those I didn't meet were a female acrobat and a Japanese woman who could not speak or understand a word of English. The extraordinary thing about his four divorces was that they were all apparently amicable. The man never paid a single dime in alimony. Of course that may have been because they were all relieved to be rid of him.

But I think he was at his happiest with the wives of his friends. Then he could just relax and be himself. He had confessed to me that he always preferred the company of women. He liked his male friends, but he generally found women more interesting than men. What's more, as he happily noted, "They smell better."

One year, he decided to visit Europe. As I recall, Germany, Ireland, and France, were on his itinerary. One day, when I went up to his house, I found him working on a newspaper ad that he intended to place in the capital cities of all three countries. He wanted to know my opinion. In it, he described himself as an eligible bachelor who was a millionaire and owned his own home. All of which was true. The part that wasn't was the part that stated this catch was in his 50s.

The plan was that if the ad worked as expected, he would receive a number of solicitations from unencumbered women who would happily pick him up at the airport, drive him around sightseeing, maybe cook him a meal, or maybe invite him to save on his hotel bills.

It sounded a little sneaky to me, but I figured any woman who would respond to such an ad had to be almost as desperate as Roger. He received scores of letters and photos, and then spent a few days deciding which of them would be the lucky winners of Roger's lottery.

Weeks later, he returned home and reported that he had had a wonderful time, but was still unmarried.

A couple of months later, he got word that the lady from Ireland was coming to the States and wondered if he would provide the same hospitality. He would, and he did. She was a nice lady, and I suspect that she had also fudged on her age when she replied to his ad.

Shortly before Roger died, he confided something to me that I had long suspected. He said, "When I was young, I kept women around for sex. When I got older, I had sex in order to keep women around."

The world lost not only one of the true eccentrics when Roger died in 1990, but perhaps the last of the great romantics.

GROUCHO WILL BE GROUCHO

I first met Groucho Marx at Nate 'n' Al's, a Beverly Hills deli down the hill from Groucho's home. I was a bit nervous, as I tended to be whenever I had occasion to conduct an interview with someone I admired.

To the extent I was a fan, it was of his radio-TV quiz show, *You Bet Your Life*, not his movies. I had never found the movies funny, aside from an occasional wisecrack penned by George S. Kaufman or Morrie Ryskind.

He was pleasant company, although I must confess I was slightly put off by his penchant for puns. An occasional pun is okay, although I've never found them to be as funny or clever as the people making them seem to believe. The real problem is that after a while, if they become incessant, you no longer feel as if you're having a conversation. Instead, you feel like a straight man to a guy who is only listening for a cue.

But at our initial meeting, Groucho, for the most part, was happy enough to recount anecdotes about the early days and to confess that he and Harpo only made some of their later movies in order to provide Chico with a pay day so that he could temporarily bail himself out of his gambling debts.

It wasn't until near the end of our lunch that I witnessed my first real Groucho moment. Out of the corner of my eye, I noticed an elderly couple spot Groucho. At least the wife did. She made a beeline for our booth. Upon arriving, she could barely contain herself. While her husband hung back a few feet, she said: "It's such a thrill to meet you. I've always been a big fan."

Groucho turned a beady eye on her and said a few of the rude things he might have said to Margaret Dumont 30 years earlier in one of the Marx Brothers movies.

But this was real life, and I'm sure I winced as Groucho said something Marxian about her age, her weight and/or her looks. But instead of being crushed, she was delighted. It was obvious that she would be dining out on this encounter, perhaps for the rest of her life.

When the couple took their leave, Groucho turned to me and said, "There, that's the second worst thing about getting old." Even though I was only in my 30s at the time, I understood that lack of sexual potency was number one. "Second worst is that when you insult people, they think you're kidding."

Over the next few years, I would see Groucho every few months for lunch. Or he would invite me to a party. I often remarked to friends that although the puns would sometimes grow tedious, I met some wonderful people through the association. I would never have met people like songwriter Harry ("Three Little Words") Ruby; Harpo's delightful widow Susan; writer-producer Nunnally (*The Grapes of Wrath*) Johnson; screenwriter Morrie (*My Man Godfrey*) Ryskind, who let me know that, prior to the famous Hollywood blacklist of the late '40s and early '50s that targeted communists, there was an earlier one conducted by the communists who ruled studio story departments that targeted conservatives such as himself.

Then there was the man I referred to as "the nice Groucho." That was Arthur Sheekman, who not only wrote some of Groucho's movies, but would often write and edit things anonymously for Groucho. Not only were they great friends, but they looked very much alike. Sheekman's advantage was that he was very kind and witty, and didn't rely on puns.

Sheekman's widow, the actress Gloria Stuart, who died at the age of 100 and made her farewell performance at age 86 playing the 101-year-old Rose Calvert in *Titanic*, once said that the only tender thing she ever heard Groucho say occurred when Arthur was very ill in the hospital and one day, while visiting, Groucho leaned over the bed and said, "Arthur, don't die before me."

Good friend that he was, Arthur hung on and died five months after Groucho.

For me, the only trouble with Groucho's parties was that people would sometimes feel called upon to sing for their supper. On one such occasion, it was George Burns. I actually had to put up with that nonsense because it was before dinner was served. At two other parties, though, the vocalizing began after the food had been served. The first time it was Theo Bikel, who had brought along his guitar; another time it was Barbra Streisand, who had brought along her larynx. Each time, I made my way quietly to the front door and slipped out.

I know that some people must be gasping in shock or horror that I would get up and leave. But my rule was to meet and speak to people at dinner parties and to keep quiet at concerts. If other people felt that singing was appropriate on any and all occasions, that was their business. But I saw no reason to encourage that sort of thing.

I would continue showing up at Groucho's home on occasion. After a while, I would find a red-headed woman who was much closer to my age than Groucho's in attendance. She didn't usually have too much to say, but she seemed to treat Groucho well, serving, so far as I could tell, as a combination secretary/caretaker.

After Groucho passed away, Erin Fleming became famous or perhaps notorious is the better word. It seems that in his will Groucho had left Erin a small house in West Hollywood. But when Groucho's son, Arthur, got wind of it, he, as the executor of Groucho's will, took her to court.

In my experience, Groucho never had a good word to say about Arthur, so I was a bit surprised that he had entrusted him with the executorship.

I followed the lawsuit in the newspaper, and what I read made me angry. For one thing, Arthur never seemed to be around when I was there, whereas I knew for a fact that Erin, working closely with Groucho's PR man, had arranged for the government of France to present Groucho with a medal for his contribution to the arts. As it was on a ribbon, I never thereafter saw Groucho without it. Once, I even saw him wearing it with his pajamas.

For another thing, Erin had encouraged Groucho to do a one-man stage show. What's more, working in concert with publicist Warren Cowan, she had helped arrange for the Motion Picture Academy to present Groucho with an honorary Oscar. Thanks to all this, I saw years roll off Groucho. He went from being an old guy that the world had passed by to being recognized and applauded. It was as if Erin had provided Groucho with a direct pipeline to the Fountain of Youth.

Something else about the lawsuit that infuriated me was reading testimony by a couple of Groucho's servants who claimed Erin had abused Groucho both verbally and physically, even claiming that on one occasion she had pushed his face into a bowl of soup. Needless to say, I never witnessed any hint of abuse or I would have stopped her and called the cops. I did hear Groucho make the occasional wisecrack at Erin's expense, but more often he was effusive -- at least effusive for Groucho -- in his praise.

It seemed to me that the servants were either lying because they'd been paid off or they were telling the truth, in which case they should have been arrested for standing by and allowing an old man, their employer no less, to be mistreated.

It finally got to be too much and I phoned Fleming's defense attorney and offered to testify.

Of course I couldn't testify to things I didn't witness, but I could at least suggest that the abuse sounded far-fetched to me. I do recall telling the court that it wasn't always easy putting up with Groucho's jibes, but that Erin Fleming, whatever her shortcomings may have been during the seven years she had devoted to Groucho, had been a boon to Groucho, making his final years a lot happier than his son had.

I summed up by saying I had read that the house was valued at $200,000 and knowing how difficult Groucho could be, if she only came away with $30,000-a-year, Groucho was getting off cheap.

But even my silver tongue wasn't enough to carry the day. Arthur and the bank came away with the house.

SNAPSHOTS

There have been many occasions when my connection to celebrities was tenuous at best, but nevertheless memorable in some way.

For instance, back when Richard Nixon was in the White House, a great deal of press attention focused on the rumor that Dr. Henry Kissinger, Nixon's chief advisor on foreign matters, was keeping company, as they say, with Hollywood tootsie Jill St. John (born Jill Oppenheim). I recall commenting that any administration that had Henry Kissinger (born Heinz Alfred Kissinger) as its resident sex symbol was in big trouble. And that was before Watergate.

Although Ms. St. John cut a dashing figure in a bikini, the only reason I agreed to have lunch with her when I was approached by her P.R. man was because I was eager to get the skinny on this odd twosome. The lady, after all, had been rumored at one time or another to have dated everyone from Frank Sinatra to Sean Connery in between marriages to Lance Reventlow, son of Barbara Hutton and heir to the Woolworth fortune, and singer Jack Jones. And now, if the media was to be believed, she was playing footsies with a guy 18 years her senior who spoke with a thick German accent and looked like an accountant with a guilty conscience.

I arrived punctually at the restaurant she had designated and then cooled my heels for half an hour. She finally breezed in, offering no apology for her tardiness, announcing, instead, that she would answer no questions about Mr. Kissinger. Because I had a fairly immediate deadline, I stuck around long enough to get a few nondescript quotes.

***

Fortunately, that wasn't the case with Alexander MacKendrick. Initially, I was delighted when invited to interview the dean of the film school at the newly established California Institute of the Arts. That wasn't because deans have any particular fascination for me, but because MacKendrick had directed some of my favorite movies, including two Alec Guinness comedies, *The Man in the White Suit* and *The Ladykillers*, and followed them up with one of my three or four all-time favorite movies, *The Sweet Smell of Success*.

No sooner had I entered his temporary office then he said, "I won't answer any questions about my past career. I will only speak about my plans for the film department."

"But the only reason you were offered the job is because of the movies you directed."

When he repeated his statement, I turned around and walked out. He had his rules, I had mine.

***

If you think that was quick, I once received a call from her P.R. man, asking if I'd care to interview Eve Arden, who was in town acting in a play. Because I had always enjoyed her wise-cracking performances in everything from *Mildred Pierce* to *Our Miss Brooks*, I agreed. At which point, her P.R. man said, "But she won't answer any questions about her past career."

I considered introducing her to Alex MacKendrick, but instead I just passed on the interview.

***

In spite of spending most of my life in the company of celebrities, I am shy by nature. So it was that once, at the opening of an art gallery, I spotted Lizabeth Scott across the room. This was some years after she had retired from the screen, but I was still intimidated by her. After all, she had usually been cast as icy cold blondes whose smoky voice could turn the hardest of men into jelly. No way was I about to approach her, even to let her know I had enjoyed her performances.

But then she opened her mouth to speak to someone and I noticed something I had never seen before. She was an adult with braces on her teeth. I was accustomed to talking to females wearing braces, but they had all been nine or ten years old at the time. With the intimidation factor gone, I hurried over, introduced myself, and made a friend for life.

Although I never mentioned to her that I had seen the issue of *Confidential* magazine years earlier that claimed she was one of Hollywood's many lesbians, she did volunteer after we'd become friends that she had retired when she did because she was getting publicity that embarrassed her family back in Scranton, PA.

She did however share anecdotes about her involvement with Hal Wallis, who had brought her to Hollywood and had her under exclusive contract for a while. She also told me she had been engaged to a Texas oil man, allegedly the love of her life, who died in a private plane crash shortly before they were to be married.

I discovered that she had been born Emma Matzo, and early on realized that a name change was in order. She had always liked the name Elizabeth, but decided it would attract more attention if she dropped the "E."

Lizabeth had gotten her first big break, appearing on Broadway with the madcap team of Olsen & Johnson in the smash hit, *Hellzapoppin'*.

Her next job was as understudy to Tallulah Bankhead in Thornton Wilder's Pulitzer Prize-winning play, *The Skin of Our Teeth*. She got the job because the producers needed to protect themselves from the temperamental Bankhead, who made a habit of threatening to walk out at a moment's notice. With Scott in the wings, Bankhead lost much of her ability to intimidate. So, instead, she took out her frustration by barking orders to the young actress, until Lizabeth stood up to her and insisted she begin saying "Please." As is often the case with bullies, once confronted they tend to back down. After that, Bankhead stopped giving orders and belatedly learned to say "Please."

What I hadn't heard until after Lizabeth died in 2015, at the age of

92, was that the short story upon which the movie *All About Eve* was based was intended to depict the story of Bankhead and Scott.

From what I know about the real story, I suspect that both Margo Channing and Eve Harrington were an amalgamation of every older and younger actress whose paths had ever crossed. I'm not just saying that because I doubt if Lizabeth had ever been quite that cut-throat about her career, but because I recall once hearing Joseph Mankiewicz, who wrote and directed the movie, say that the movie was originally supposed to star Claudette Colbert as Margo. But when Ms. Colbert suddenly became unavailable, and with a start date looming just days away, the studio signed Bette Davis.

Mankiewicz said he never changed a word of dialogue to accommodate his new lead, but observed that if Colbert had played the role, everyone would have assumed he had based the character on the more ladylike stage actress Ilka Chase. But because the earthier Bette Davis was the one to suggest that her party guests fasten their seat belts because "it's going to be a bumpy night!" in that familiar throaty voice, people assumed Margo was based on Tallulah Bankhead.

I knew that Lizabeth was in her 90s, but because she remained as svelte and as straight-back as she'd been in her 20s, and with that same remarkable voice, it came as a shock when I heard of her passing.

In retrospect, I could only be grateful that 50 years earlier, she'd finally decided her teeth needed straightening.

***

One of my briefest encounters took place in a Santa Monica deli called Zucky's. I was having lunch with a friend when he looked past me and across the aisle. "Isn't that Dana Andrews?" he asked.

I turned and looked over my left shoulder. It was Dana Andrews. I assumed the older woman sitting with her back to me was Mrs. Andrews.

He had always been a favorite of mine, at least in the 1940s before his battle with alcoholism had become public knowledge. I had always thought it was a disgrace that he had never even been nominated for an Academy Award; not for *The Ox-Bow Incident*, not for *Laura*, not even for *The Best Years of Our Lives*, which saw the Oscar go to Fredric March, but should have gone to Dana Andrews because his performance was far more nuanced and demanding.

By the time my friend and I spotted him, the world of films and the world in general had pretty much passed him by, and he, who had been one of the major stars at 20th Century-Fox, had wound up working in low-budget fare that bore titles like *Hot Rods to Hell*, *The Frozen Dead*, and *Curse of the Demon*, before tossing in the towel and getting into real estate.

My friend said he'd like to tell Andrews that *A Walk in the Sun* was one of his very favorite films, but was too shy. As we were just finishing up I said we'd stop at his booth on the way out and we'd both tell him.

Although Dana Andrews had been known as an actor who didn't often display his emotions on screen, there was no concealing his joy at being recognized and praised by a couple of guys who had been kids when he'd been at the top of his game. Judging by the smile on his wife's face, he wasn't alone.

I realized then that it isn't necessary to ask someone you admire for their autograph. Just mention that you admire their work. I suspect you will remember it long after the signature would have faded on the page.

***

One day, I received a call from Jack Klugman, whom I had never met. It seemed he had an idea for a sitcom and needed someone to write a script. The network had suggested me.

In a way, I was a little bit surprised to have been called. That's because for some reason I couldn't imagine, Klugman had declared war on the Writers Guild. He had dismissed its members as hacks who weren't good enough to write for his dramatic series about a medical examiner, *Quincy, M.E.* In more than one interview, he had invited college students to submit scripts.

Perhaps that plan hadn't worked out as well as he had hoped.

In any case, I had a meeting with him, his manager, and a CBS executive. Although *Quincy* was a hit and Klugman wouldn't be free to star in another series for at least two or three more years, and although he insisted he would not be starring in this other series even if it sold, it certainly sounded like it was tailor-made for him. In fact, it was reminiscent of *The Odd Couple* on TV, but without Felix Unger.

The show he had in mind would revolve around a sportswriter, much like the Oscar Madison he had portrayed opposite Tony Randall. He'd be rude, slovenly, and barely housebroken.

Because of something he has written in his column, the newspaper he works for is once again being threatened with a lawsuit. The paper decides he needs to be reined in. The solution is to have him write the advice to the lovelorn column, at least for a while, at least until he learns to behave himself or until the series ends its run.

After I signed the contract I had one more meeting, which took place with just Klugman at his Malibu beachside condo. I had heard that Klugman liked to gamble, but I had no idea. When I arrived he had competitions of one sort or another going on five or six different TV sets. They were tuned to football games, horse races and, for all I know, a chess tournament. Jack had money riding on all of them.

He explained once again what he had in mind for the character, and I went home to write a script.

The writing went well, but that's the only thing that did. Although everyone insisted they loved the script, my check didn't arrive in timely fashion. Because I was writing this for Klugman's production company, it was Klugman who had to pay me. He had to, but he didn't.

According to the rules of the Writer's Guild, he had only so many weeks to cough up the money before penalties began to accrue. But still he didn't send me a check. Worse yet, I couldn't reach him by phone.

Perhaps he'd taken a much bigger hit on that chess tournament than I'd imagined.

I finally contacted his manager to complain. "What? You don't trust us?"

"How can I trust you when you don't pay me?"

"Fine. If that's the way you are, come to my house. I think I have $7,000 in my safe."

"You owe me a lot more than that. Keep your $7,000 and just tell your client to pay me what the contract requires him to pay me."

A week or so later, the check arrived. But my troubles were only beginning.

When you're a member of the WGA, you're required to pay dues of either $25-a-quarter if you haven't had any earnings, or 1½% of whatever you do earn during the period.

So when the quarter ended, I sent the appropriate amount to the Guild.

The next thing I knew, I was being brought up on charges!

It seems that Klugman's company was not a signatory to the Guild. Not only was my ignorance of this fact not a defense, it was held against me. I should have checked, I was told.

But, I explained, the CBS executive had been present at the meeting. In fact, it had taken place in his office. Why would I think to check with the Guild? The folks at CBS knew I was a member of the Guild and I knew that they wouldn't be in business with a writer who wasn't in the WGA.

Although this might sound like a trivial matter, it wasn't. The mere fact that I had worked for a non-signatory was sufficient reason for them to expel me from the Guild and, for good measure, fine me the entire amount I had finally been paid.

There is, I'm sure, only one thing that saved me. And, no, for once it wasn't my good-looks and charm that carried the day.

It was the fact that Klugman had slandered the Guild writers once too often. They weren't about to let him be responsible for ruining a writer's career.

So, thank you, Jack, for being such a schmuck.

***

When I went to interview George Carlin, I didn't know what to expect. Although, being a baseball fan, I had appreciated the bit in which he compared baseball to football and displayed his bias for baseball, I thought his reliance on obscenities in his comedy was an obvious form of pandering to his college audiences. It didn't help when he would suggest that it was a form of homage to the late Lenny Bruce. I had seen Bruce perform live twice in my life, and neither time had he elicited a smile, let alone a laugh.

Bruce, himself, was a bit of a fraud, pretending he was freeing up the language and letting it breathe. Anyone who had ever read Herman Miller or *From Here to Eternity* or even Erskine Caldwell, had already come across all the words that Bruce seemed to think he'd invented. All he had done was introduce them into a public venue, with the result that in no time at all, every other second-rate standup comic would be employing them to garner cheap laughs from ignoramuses.

Carlin was polite and well-spoken, and never uttered a single profanity. But the thing I gave him the most credit for was that he had managed to totally re-invent himself, as few public figures ever had. One who comes to mind was Mike Wallace. He had been a game show host, but he so desperately wanted to be a newsman that he had walked away from untold millions of dollars that await anyone who manages to get himself on the short list of people who can host TV quiz shows and game shows.

Another was Dick Powell. During the 30s, he was constantly on the list of top 10 moneymakers. In role after role he would portray some version of a male ingénue. Sometimes he would sing in a voice a castrato would envy in corny musicals and sometimes he would be the asexual romantic lead in equally cornball comedies.

But, then, one day he decided he'd had enough of being pigeonholed as wimps and totally converted his image by playing a series of tough guys in the likes of *Cornered; Murder, My Sweet; Rogue's Regiment;* and *To the Ends of the Earth.*

In much the same way, Carlin started out as a very successful comedian who wore skinny ties and buttoned-down shirts and told suburban-type jokes about commuter trains and crab grass. He put his entire career on the line when he went from being a comic who was deemed acceptable for Ed Sullivan's family audience, to being a potty-mouthed stoner who would have been right at home performing in burlesque houses, smokers, and college frat houses.

In the end, it wasn't his comedy I admired, it was the courage he exhibited in undertaking such a radical metamorphosis.

***

During the time when I was being actively discriminated against because I had had the bad taste of living past the age of 50, which in terms of TV writers, is deemed long past shelf life, I was invited to New York to appear on *Primetime Live* along with Jimmy Komack and a couple of other older creative types who'd been put out to pasture by the youth-obsessed nutburgers at the networks.

They fed us well and put us up at a nice hotel. Best of all, we would be interviewed on camera by the diva herself, Diane Sawyer.

The interviews all went off very well, if I do say so myself. In fact, if I do say so myself, I thought I did a particularly good job of displaying a stiff upper lip by being charming and amusing about a really lousy reality; the reality that in a business that never stops harping about a blacklist that ended over 60 years ago, it was still okay to blacklist people, based not on their allegiance to a foreign tyranny, but simply on their age.

As we were wrapping up, I asked Ms. Sawyer how old she was. Although she certainly looked younger than any of us, I was surprised when she told me the truth and I discovered that she was only a few years younger than we were.

"Well, no wonder you were so anxious to do this story," I remarked.

Think what you will, but that wasn't why the piece never aired. We were pre-empted because Jackie Kennedy Onassis took the least opportune time imaginable to die, and it was decided that her passing took precedence over the plight of older writers. But that's TV for you.

***

By the time I met Burt Reynolds he had already become the top box office star in America, but he was still sharing a bachelor pad with his best pal, movie director Hal Needham.

Like everyone else who ever interviewed Reynolds, I found him outgoing and amusing. But I'm afraid that when he tried to prove himself just a regular down-to-earth guy, I found it rather ingenuous.

He boasted: "I'm probably the only leading man in Hollywood who will ever admit to being less than six feet tall."

"How tall are you?" I asked.

"I'm 5-10 and a half."

Mentioning that half inch seemed to slightly offset his boast.

But he seemed to be a nice guy and I didn't push it. Still, I couldn't help noticing that the cowboy boots he was wearing had two inch heels.

***

I probably never anticipated an interview more than the one I had with Stan Laurel at his apartment in Santa Monica. I had always regarded Laurel and Hardy as the quintessential comedy team. For one thing, they conveyed a genuine warmth; for another, neither was, strictly speaking, a straight man in the tradition of Bud Abbott or Dean Martin. Both Laurel and Hardy were funny, with both being knuckleheads, but with one, Hardy, assuming he was the brains of the outfit.

As the interview turned out, I came away with little more than the ability to say that I had met the comic genius.

42

The problem was that Laurel had fairly recently sat down with John McCabe, who was working on a full-blown bio to be titled *Mr. Laurel and Mr. Hardy*, and Laurel refused to share with me any of the things he had told Mr. McCabe. I tried to assure him that I was only interviewing him for my college paper, and that whatever appeared in a short article in the UCLA *Daily Bruin* would do nothing to cramp McCabe's potential book sales, but he stuck to his guns.

Clearly, he felt he owed me something because he proceeded to put on an LP of some English music hall comic I had never heard of and hoped to never hear of again. Although Laurel insisted the guy was hysterical, I failed to see it or, rather, hear it. Amazing how time seems to slow down when you're having a really terrible time. I could have sworn the LP lasted six hours. Good manners, I felt, demanded that I stick it through to the end.

But I found it hard to believe that the man who had thought up most of the comedy bits for the team 30 years before while his partner spent his own off-hours at the race track, could think the guy on the record was even slightly amusing.

The one thing I did discover was that the reason that Laurel and his wife had moved from their home in Malibu to the second-floor apartment overlooking the Pacific was that the TV reception in Malibu was just awful. As a result, he could no longer stroll down memory lane watching old Laurel and Hardy comedies.

***

While at UCLA I also interviewed Dalton Trumbo, one of the Hollywood 10 who had gone to jail for taking the 5th when called before a congressional committee and asked to testify about fellow members of the Communist party.

Although Trumbo had once been the highest-paid screenwriter at MGM, having *A Guy Named Joe*, *Kitty Foyle*, and *Our Vines Have Tender Grapes*, to his credit, he had been forced to use fronts and pseudonyms for several years after getting out of prison. Two of those movies, *Roman Holiday* and *The Brave One*, had won Oscars for their scripts.

When I paid a visit to his home, he was about to bust out of the black list big time by writing and getting screen credit for *Spartacus* and *Exodus*. Kirk Douglas and Otto Preminger, two of Hollywood's more prominent liberals, competed to get the credit for being the first to hire Trumbo. As I recall, one of them hired Trumbo first, but the other one was the first to get his movie completed and into the theaters, so each got to share in the glory of hiring an unrepentant communist who had tithed a portion of his salary to Joseph Stalin and his coterie of butchers.

Although legend has it that Trumbo always wrote while soaking in his bathtub, I fortunately got to conduct the interview while he was fully clothed. I also saw that his approach to scriptwriting was to pin dozens of index cards, apparently representing various scenes and passages of dialogue, to a board and to then move them around until he had them organized to his satisfaction.

To me, it suggested a shopkeeper's approach to the art of screenwriting, an approach that struck me as the equivalent of painting by the numbers.

I came away thinking Trumbo had written a character and then set about performing it in real life. Everything from his slightly English accent to his ivory cigarette holder to the great white hunter outfit he had adopted along the way, seemed to be a role this ex-baker from a small town in Colorado had staked out early and made his own.

***

I had not wished to interview Andy Warhol, but a mutual friend had kept after me, insisting it would work out well for both of us. I accepted that I would get an article out of it, but, for the life of me, I couldn't imagine how it would benefit Warhol to have someone, who thought his movies were boring and that his canvases were a contrivance created by New York's art critics and wealthy collectors to make a killing off this fraud, meet and write about him.

But as a favor to our friend, I showed up at the Beverly Wilshire Hotel in Beverly Hills, where Warhol and his troupe of freaks and no-talents had taken up temporary residence. When I entered the room, it was jammed. I know that two of his "super stars," Viva and Ultra Violet, were there, but I didn't recognize the others, except for my friend.

He introduced me to Warhol, who seemed even less interested in meeting me than I was in meeting him. Over the next hour or so, I asked him a number of questions. He answered some of them, but always with a "yes" or "no" answer, even when it was a question to which either "yes" or "no" made not the slightest bit of sense. It was something like trying to carry on a conversation with Chatty Cathy, except that Warhol didn't come with a ring pull. In addition to which, he would take so long to respond, that I couldn't be sure what my question had been or if he was merely responding to a question floating around in his own head.

When I finally gave up and took my leave, my writer friend followed me down the corridor to the elevator. Although all these years later, I can't even recall what Warhol's voice sounded like, I still recall our mutual friend telling me in all seriousness that Warhol really liked me.

"And how do you know this?" I asked, as the elevator doors began to close between us.

"Because he never opens up the way he opened up to you."

***

The only similar situation I ever found myself in was when another friend, a show biz publicity man, invited me to his Sunset Strip office to meet his latest client.

When I entered Joe's office, his client, a wild-eyed, wild-haired, individual of indeterminate gender was seated on a couch. I found the

45

only place left for me to sit down was on the same small couch, not nearly far enough away from Tiny Tim to suit me.

After he had answered every conceivable question I could come up with, Joe told Tiny Tim to sing for me. In case I haven't mentioned it, I don't like being sung to. But that was all the encouragement Tiny needed. The next thing I knew he had opened up a cloth bag that had been lying at his feet. For a moment I was relieved that it wasn't a snake or someone's body part. It was, of all things, a ukulele. Within seconds, I found myself wishing it had been a snake.

Here was Tiny Tim sitting two feet away, strumming and crooning *Tiptoe Through the Tulips* to me. The thing about being serenaded is that it's rude to look away. So I had nowhere else to look but straight at Tiny Tim.

It's been many years, but the experience still leaves scars.

Worst of all, when I turned in the piece, my editor wouldn't run it. I forget his rationale, but perhaps he felt that I hadn't engaged in doing an actual interview with a show business talent, but had merely sought out an escaped loon to ridicule.

It was only about a month later, after *Life* magazine had devoted a couple of pages to this phenomenon who was taking the nation by storm, that I could finally get the piece published in the *L.A. Times*. Of course by then it was old news and I could no longer take credit for warning America what was on the horizon.

Some months later, I was in that same office one afternoon when a client of my friend phoned him from Lake Tahoe. It was Bill Cosby calling to say that he would be flying into L.A. late that night after wrapping up his engagement at Harrah's and wanted his publicist to line up a girl.

Until then, I had no idea that part of my friend's responsibilities was to provide prostitutes for his clientele. When he promised Cosby to get right on it, it ended our friendship. I suppose even pimps need friends, but I saw no reason to fill that need.

But at least I wasn't blindsided years later when "America's favorite dad" turned out to be someone who drugged and raped helpless women.

***

One of my favorite interviews was with Art Linkletter. We had arranged a time for me to visit him at his office, but the day before it was set to take place I received a call from his secretary. It seems that Mr. Linkletter was off on a skiing vacation and the conditions were so perfect, he had decided to stay another week.

Frankly, I was surprised that at his age, which was then in his 80s, he was still risking life and limb on the slopes.

But the week passed, as weeks often tend to do, and I found myself sitting across the desk from a guy who looked like he might be 60.

He shared with me the fact that he had been an orphan baby in a small town in Canada when he'd been adopted by a minister and his wife from San Diego.

He went to college with the idea of becoming a teacher. To earn his keep, he worked at a radio station as an announcer. By the time he graduated and went to be interviewed by the school superintendent, the Depression had hit and they could only offer him $120-a-month. Because he was making $125 at the radio station, he turned it down.

He admitted that if the teaching job had paid the extra $5, he would have taken it. Still, he did confess that once he had decided to stick with radio, he was confident he would achieve great success. But just how, he had no idea. "After all, I wasn't an actor, I couldn't sing, and I didn't tell jokes particularly well."

So what happened?

"One day, a guy down in Texas sent in an audition tape. They were a series of man-on-the-street interviews he had conducted, and when I heard it, the biggest light bulb in the world went on over my head. I can do that! I can talk to people."

And talk he did. Over the next 60 years he seemed to constantly be talking to tens of thousands of men, women, and kids.

There came a time when he was on both radio and TV on a daily basis, broadcasting 10 hours a week. "Some of my friends would ask me if I ever had time to see my wife and kids. What they didn't understand was that I never used a script, so there was nothing to rehearse. When I was doing 10 hours a week, except for the drive time, I was working 10 hours a week."

Towards the end of the interview, I mentioned that he was rumored to own most of Australia as well as several large portions of the United States, and asked him why he still felt it necessary to get involved in so many business ventures.

"It's not about the money," he admitted. In fact, when I had asked him at what point he realized he was financially secure and would never need to work another day in his life, he nearly knocked me off my chair when he said, "1947." You see it was now 1996.

So why, I wondered, why was he still so deeply engrossed in making deals? "Just for the satisfaction. You get an idea or someone brings you an idea, and you work to develop it and bring it to fruition. That's the real satisfaction. The money is just a way of keeping score."

As a parting question, I asked Art Linkletter what was the best thing about being as rich as Art Linkletter. He said, "If someone comes into my office and I don't like him, I can toss him out on his ear."

I was leaving anyway.

***

One of my bigger surprises took place when I showed up to interview Zsa Zsa Gabor. Her maid pointed me in the direction of what I took to be the den. It was the den, but when I opened the door, I found Zsa Zsa dressed for the boudoir in a flowing negligee.

I immediately felt over-dressed, but, then, unlike Hugh Hefner, I wasn't in the habit of wearing pajamas on the job.

Just for the record, nothing unseemly took place. Which I admit is unfortunate because it would no doubt have helped book sales if something had.

The most memorable thing I recall of the event is that weeks later, on the Sunday morning the interview appeared, I received a phone call. It was Zsa Zsa's daughter, Francesca Hilton, letting me know that her mother would like me to bring over 50 copies of the newspaper.

I explained that I wasn't a delivery boy and that her mother would have to go out and buy them.

In the hope it will hype sales, I confess that when I received the call, I was wearing nothing but my pajamas.

WHEN A CIGAR'S MORE THAN JUST A SMOKE

I never would have dreamed that I'd ever have fond feelings for George Burns. That's because the first time I met him was at a small dinner party at Groucho Marx's home. There were only about ten or eleven of us sitting around in Groucho's den, broken down in conversational groups of two or three having pre-dinner cocktails when Burns suddenly stepped to the middle of the floor and, without preamble or putting it to a vote, started performing one of his patter songs.

I had been speaking to screenwriter Norman Panama when the nonsense song began, and I recall looking at him, questioning if this was typical of Burns. His shrug suggested that it was all too typical.

Therefore, when a friend of mine, a PR man named Arnold Lipsman, called me a couple of years later, asking if I would care to interview Burns for my Sunday column in the *L.A. Times*, I said I'd pass. Arnold explained that Burns wasn't his client, that White Owl Cigars was, but that White Owl was sponsoring his show at the Century City theater.

I told Lipsman I didn't care. I wasn't interested in interviewing the boor.

Lipsman, not one to take no for an answer, told me I could conduct the interview over lunch at the legendary Hillcrest Country Club, the one Jewish country club in Los Angeles that boasted a typical lunch crowd that included Jack Benny, Groucho Marx, Milton Berle, George Jessel, Jack Carter, and apparently George Burns.

I still held out, pointing out that I lived in the San Fernando Valley and not even the idea of having lunch under the same roof as those guys was worth a 40-mile round trip. That's when Lipsman, who knew me all too well, played his trump card. He said he was sure the cigar

51

company would spring for a car and driver. I caved like a cheap beach chair.

The car came and I went. One-on-one and without the singing, I found Burns funny, charming, and warm-hearted.

After the article ran, an ecstatic Lipsman told me he was leaving four tickets for me at the theater. Even though it meant doing my own driving and having to listen to Helen Reddy sing *I Am Woman, Hear Me Roar*, as his opening act, I accepted the offer.

Considering that he must have been well up in his 80s, Burns and his cigar were very funny. In spite of the drive, I was glad I came. That was until the wife of the friend I had invited to join me and my wife insisted on meeting Burns.

I tried to beg off, but soon my wife joined in, leaving me no choice.

Once we went backstage, it was as if we had entered the catacombs of some ancient city. Part catacombs, part maze. Corridors led off in all directions. And did I mention that it was like a steam bath?

Finally, like Moses finding the Promised Land, we actually stumbled upon George's dressing room. It was packed to the brim with sweaty bodies. But once I managed to haul my guests through the two rooms and out the back door, I discovered that none of the bodies belonged to Burns.

Frankly, I was relieved. After all, I had only spent an hour with him. It was already nearing 11 p.m., Burns was in his 80s and he had just finished an exhausting two hours on stage. I could imagine introducing him to my wife and my two guests and having him say, "Fine. Now who the heck are you?!"

Which is why only three of us were disappointed not to find him and why only three of us were delighted when we turned a corner on our way out, and up ahead about 100 yards, we spotted the back of a young woman -- his caretaker, I presume -- helping a hunched over old man make his way to the exit.

As we increased our gait, I remember thinking -- hoping -- that there was no possible way we were going to catch up with them. But it was as if they had begun walking backwards. Within seconds, perhaps

20 at most, we were upon them. Tentatively, I tapped Mr. Burns on the shoulder. Slowly he turned, so slowly that my blood had a chance to freeze.

He looked up, smiled and said, "Burt…how nice to see you again."

I could have kissed him.

JACK'S WILD

When I read that Jack Elam had died at the age of 82, I couldn't believe it. Okay, I believed it. But I didn't like it. The world can ill-afford to lose the likes of Jack.

I got to know Jack back in the 70s when we both played in a weekly poker game. What I remember best was how eerie it was sitting across the table from Jack and that wild left eye of his, trying to figure out if he was looking at me or at three other guys.

A remarkable thing about the man was that he brought a family-sized thermos bottle to every game. It was filled with bourbon. You could always tell when we were playing our last hand of the evening because Jack would just be pouring out the last drop. It wasn't just in front of the camera that his timing was impeccable. To Jack's credit, whatever it might have been doing to his liver, the booze never seemed to affect his behavior. Even after five hours, you would have thought he'd been lapping up spring water.

He was a terrific poker player. But he really made his reputation playing liar's poker on movie and TV sets. He was legendary at the game. To hear his fellow actors describe it, I suspect with some exaggeration, he made more dough that way than by acting. And, best of all, he didn't have to pay an agent's commission on his winnings.

The Wednesday game consisted mainly of actors and myself. Regulars included Dick and Vince Van Patten, Don Galloway, Roger Price, Ned Wertimer and Ronny Cox, and, on occasion, Allan Miller, Gene Troobnik, and Lee Majors.

The game took place at Wertimer's Studio City condo. Specifically, it took place on his second story loft. It was in that small space that the poker table was wedged. As a result, only two players had easy access to the stairs if they needed to use the ground floor facilities. If any of the other five players needed to heed the call of nature, two or three players had to get up and move their chairs and themselves. I mention the physical set-up because it played such an essential role in my most cherished memory of the dearly departed.

The year, I believe, was 1974. We had a new guy in the game that evening. His name was Richard Dreyfuss. He had made a few movies already, most notably *The Apprenticeship of Duddy Kravitz* and *American Graffiti*. It happened, luckily for him, that he had one of the two seats with easy access to the stairway, whereas Jack was wedged into one of the corners.

Ours was not a big game, you should understand. In their game, the likes of Steve Martin and Danny Melnick played for thousands. We played for slightly lower stakes. If you had a truly terrible night, you might lose two hundred bucks.

We were an hour and a half into the game when, suddenly, Mr. Dreyfuss announced, "That's it, gentlemen." He thereupon wrote out a check for about sixty dollars, stood up, brushed his hands together like a Vegas dealer going on a break, and skipped down the stairs.

I looked across the table at Jack. He looked like a cartoon character. A very angry cartoon character. I had never seen such disgust and outrage in a human face before. Veins were popping out of his neck in places where veins don't usually exist. His face had gone crimson. I was surprised not to see smoke shooting out of his nose and ears. At the same time, he was moving his mouth, but no actual words were coming out. Only noises and a little bit of spittle.

When we heard the sound of the door being closed downstairs, it seemed to act as a release on Jack. A flood of indescribable profanity came gushing forth. It was as if Vesuvius had erupted, and instead of lava, obscenities flowed out over the countryside.

Although the spirit of the words was clear enough, only some of them were actually intelligible. It seems that Elam and Dreyfuss had the same agent; that Dreyfuss was presently on hiatus from *Jaws* while Steven Spielberg and his associates got the kinks out of their mechanical shark; that Dreyfuss was getting paid $250,000 for the movie; and that he had already signed to star in his next one for a cool million.

The fact that a wealthy young man was leaving a game short-handed because he was losing sixty dollars was an offense to everything Jack held sacred. If it had been a western, Elam would have gunned him down, and the jury would have carried Jack out of the courtroom on their shoulders.

But, unfortunately, it was real life. Still, if Richard had had to get by Jack to leave the game, I guarantee he'd never have reached those stairs alive. By this time, I'm sure that somewhere Jack is playing liar's poker for halos, harps, and wings, and that St. Peter is running around in his skivvies, saying, "I was so sure he was bluffing."

However, Dreyfuss and I were to cross paths, more or less, one more time. Some years later, I read that, while under the influence of cocaine, he had crashed his car on a canyon road not too far from where I was living.

I assumed that our having sat across the poker table that one time, however briefly, gave me reason enough to write him a letter while he was recuperating in the hospital.

I told him that if, in spite of fame and fortune, he found he required cocaine to help him deal with the anguish of everyday life, he should kill himself quickly. I suggested he use a gun. That way, I pointed out, he wouldn't risk wiping out an entire family the next time he had a crash on a winding road.

I didn't hear back, but I didn't really expect to.

However, a few years later, I saw Dreyfuss being interviewed on TV. When the talk show host asked him how he had managed to break his drug habit, Dreyfuss said it was all the result of an experience he had had while lying in the hospital, recovering from his self-inflicted injuries.

He said he was visited by the vision of a little girl dressed in white, and realized she was the child he was destined to have, but who might never be born if he didn't clean up his act.

As I recall, the host and the audience were moved by his story.

I, on the other hand, was moved to sit down and write him another letter. I reminded him that I had written him an earlier letter in which I pointed out that, thanks to his stupidity, he could easily have wiped out an actual family and not merely the cockamamie vision of an unborn child.

To his credit, this time he wrote back. I wasn't too surprised that Dreyfuss let me know he preferred his version.

AT A WIT'S END

When I began, in 1967, to write a weekly humor column for the *L.A. Times*, I decided I would use the gig to meet people I had long admired. My plan was to use an interview as a jumping off place for the humor.

One of the people I had targeted was Oscar Levant. Although I first became aware of him through his recording of Gershwin's "Rhapsody in Blue," I had come to know him from his semi-autobiographical performances in *Cobweb*, *An American in Paris*, and *Band Wagon*, together with his appearances on Jack Paar's late night talk show and his own L.A.-based TV show, which had been co-hosted by his wife June.

Somehow, I found out his address and sent him a letter requesting an interview, but he never replied. But one Sunday night, at a party hosted by Dwight Whitney, a friend and, as the west coast editor of TV Guide, my occasional employer, I met Al Burton.

Mr. Burton had produced Levant's TV show. When I explained my dilemma, he gave me Levant's phone number, explaining that Levant rarely responded to letters.

Being by nature a very shy person, I was reluctant to follow up. But after I'd had a couple of drinks, I managed to overcome my inhibitions, went into the other room and made the call.

I almost hoped he wouldn't answer, but he did. That very familiar cranky voice said, "Yeah, who is it?"

I identified myself and explained that I was hoping to interview him for my column.

He said, "Why would anyone want to talk to me? I don't remember anything. It would be a complete waste of time."

I told him that my time wasn't that precious and I was willing to risk wasting a bit of it.

He then said, "Why should I talk to you?"

Without thinking about it, I replied: "Because when one Jewish neurotic asks another for a favor, he doesn't take no for an answer."

Apparently, it was the right answer. He agreed to see me on Tuesday. But before hanging up, he said, "But you need to bring me a couple of tranquilizers."

Great. I, who had never taken anything stronger than an aspirin had to hunt up two tranquilizers. I spent a good portion of Monday calling everyone I knew. Finally, I struck gold. Or, if not gold, at least Miltown.

I showed up punctually at the Levant home on Roxbury Drive, in Beverly Hills, and was greeted at the door by June and Oscar, who was dressed in pajamas and a bathrobe even though it was two in the afternoon. In the remaining four years of his life, I must have visited at least two dozen times and except for one Christmas party for which he wore a blue suit, I never saw him dressed any other way.

When we moved into the living room, which was roughly 40 feet long and 20 feet wide, we took the same seats we would take on every subsequent visit. I only mention it because it was the very worst seating arrangement one could have imagined.

The layout of the room had a long sofa and coffee table along the east wall. At the far north end of the coffee table was an easy chair. On the west side of the room were French doors leading to the garden. There was a straight back chair in front of one of the doors. In other words, once we were seated, I was in the easy chair, June to my right at the end of the sofa, Oscar in the chair on the other side of the room, his back to the garden, facing June and my left profile. This would have been an awkward set-up in any house with any three people, but it was beyond awkward in this household. That's because June was hard of hearing and Oscar was paranoid. Thus, if I turned to my left and spoke to Oscar, June couldn't hear what I was saying. If I turned to my right and spoke to her, Oscar became anxious, wondering what we were plotting.

One might well wonder why I kept going back. It's because my host was so fascinating, not to mention hilarious. You must keep in mind that in spite of his warning me that he couldn't remember anything, he seemed to have forgotten nothing. And because his encyclopedic knowledge included music, both popular and classic, movies, baseball, and history, coupled with the fact that he had known or worked with everyone from Fred Astaire and Gene Kelly to Arnold Schoenberg and the Gershwins, time spent in Oscar's company was so delightful, that after a visit, I always felt as if I had managed to sneak into the best show in town without having to purchase a ticket.

Oscar had not only been the most popular concert pianist in America whose version of "Rhapsody in Blue" had been at one time the world's best-selling instrumental recording; but he had been a panel member of radio's highbrow quiz show, *Information Please*, and a best-selling author of such autobiographical tomes as *A Smattering of Ignorance*, *The Unimportance of Being Oscar*, and *The Memoirs of an Amnesiac.*

As our interview was coming to an end, it seemed he had forgotten about the tranquilizers. But he had merely been biding his time. As soon as June got up to answer the phone, Oscar shot across the room as if he'd been spring-loaded. "Where are they?"

I was so shocked by his sprightliness, I actually had no idea what he was talking about.

"The tranquilizers!"

I reached into my pocket and handed them over, feeling very much like a drug dealer. Having had no experience with tranquilizers, I had no idea if I was playing a role in a suicide plot. But a deal is a deal.

Oscar shoved the pills in the pocket of his bathrobe and scurried back to his chair. Months later, he would have occasion to tell me that although he took over 140 pills of one kind or another every day -- and I had worried myself sick about handing over a couple of mild tranquilizers! -- June had the key to his medicine cabinet. "You can't imagine what that does to your manhood."

When it was time for me to leave, Oscar and June showed me to the door. He invited me to return whenever I felt like it, which made me feel very good. But he then turned to June and said, "You know, he looks just like a young me."

As I went out the door, I tried to convince myself that was meant as a compliment. I mean, as impressive as his mind and his resume were, he did somewhat resemble a rather unhappy beagle. But having said that, I must say that when he smiled, years disappeared from his face and he looked absolutely boyish.

As I discovered over time, he smiled quite often, especially when he delivered an amusing line, and that was the case even when he was merely delivering a line I had already heard, such as his remarking about Doris Day that he knew her before she was a virgin.

Something I had noticed during the first visit was that Oscar always held a cigarette in his right hand. For all I knew, it could have been the same cigarette because he never lit it. The other thing was that every so often, without warning, he would throw his head back as far as his neck would allow and open his mouth as if to scream, but no sound would emerge. After a couple of seconds, he would resume our conversation.

I couldn't bring myself to ask him about it, worried it would embarrass him. It probably took me at least a year before I worked up the nerve. As he once again picked up the conversation where he had left off, I asked him what he was experiencing when he did it.

"When I do what?"

That took me aback. He didn't sound as if he was putting me on and he wasn't smiling. Was it conceivable he was unaware of what just might be the largest and most elaborate tic in history?

I tried to describe what I saw, but he seemed totally mystified, so I had no option but to mimic what I had seen him do perhaps 50 times. I tossed my head back and opened my mouth wide in a silent scream. When I looked back at Oscar, his eyes were staring at me. I couldn't determine the exact emotion, but fear and shock were certainly involved.

"I do that?!"

"Yes, every so often. I assumed you were in pain."

He told me there was no pain involved and until now nobody had ever mentioned it.

That was a relief, and in the future I no longer worried that he was suffering the torments of the damned.

One aspect of the living room I neglected to mention was that about 10 feet behind my chair was a closed door. For years, I would occasionally wonder what it led to, but never bothered to ask. I assumed it was closed for a reason. But one afternoon, Oscar suddenly sprang up and said, "Come on."

He hurried over to the door and I followed. The room, I discovered, housed a grand piano. Oscar sat down and began to play Gershwin's "Concerto in F" like a man possessed. I am not a music savant, but it sounded wonderful. But after 10 minutes, Oscar suddenly slammed down the key guard, stood up and announced, "I told you I couldn't play!"

He never had, but once I had asked him if he ever played, if only for his own enjoyment, and he had simply said, "No."

I derived a great deal of pleasure from our conversations, and took it as the highest possible compliment when something I said actually got a laugh. But the good would occasionally come with a price. No, never again a tranquilizer. But because I wrote for the *Times*, he came to see me as something of a conduit. Once, for instance, he wanted to see a movie in Westwood and asked me to call the theater manager and arrange for him to get a pass. I had to explain that I didn't even work for the newspaper, that I was merely a freelancer, albeit one who wrote for the paper on a regular basis, and that I had far less influence on a theater manager than he would.

Another time, he phoned me at home and complained that his newspaper hadn't yet been delivered. I explained that delivering the newspaper didn't fall within my extremely small sphere of influence, but as it was only 3 a.m., he might consider giving the delivery guy another few hours to complete his rounds.

Fortunately, I used to be given to keeping very late hours.

One morning in August of 1972, June was leaving the house to buy a baby gift for my son who was about to be born. On the front path, she ran into Candace Bergen who, in her occasional role as a journalist, was showing up to interview Oscar for some magazine.

June explained that Oscar was taking a nap. She let Candace into the house and then went upstairs to wake him up. She couldn't. Oscar died on the morning of August 14th at the age of 65.

My son Max was born three days later. He never did receive his gift.

His loss was nothing compared to my own.

SNAPSHOTS II

At times during my life as an interviewer, certain moments stand out more clearly than others. One such took place when I was having lunch with the legendary Mervyn LeRoy, who had started out as a movie actor in 1922, but soon turned to producing and directing. Over the course of the next 40 years, he would play a major role in turning out the likes of *Little Caesar*, *I Am a Fugitive from a Chain Gang*, *Gold Diggers of 1933*, *The Wizard of Oz*, *Quo Vadis? The Bad Seed*, *Mr. Roberts*, and *Gypsy*.

Mr. LeRoy was very cordial and things were going along swimmingly until I happened to ask him to compare producing and directing. I believe I asked him from which pursuit he derived the greater satisfaction. Instead of just answering the question, he said, displaying the sort of false modesty Hollywood is known for: "Well, the most important element in any movie is the script. First comes the word. Without the writer, you don't have a movie."

Of course that's the same answer Hollywood big wigs have been delivering down through the decades, except when the members of the WGA periodically go on strike to demand a slightly larger fraction of the money that's regularly paid to actors, directors and producers.

But I didn't mention any of this to Mervyn LeRoy. Instead, I said, "That makes sense. So, over the years, which writers have you enjoyed working with the most?" I swear I never imagined it would constitute a gotcha question.

You would have thought I was Alex Trebek and the only thing standing between *Jeopardy!* contestant LeRoy and $100,000 was telling me to the exact mile the distance between the earth and the moon.

He furrowed his brow, he gazed at the ceiling. He shut his eyes as he searched his brain for a single name. But he searched in vain.

Finally, he gave up. "When I get back to my office, I'll send you a list."

I assured him it wouldn't be necessary. When I got home, I explained, I could look them up.

***

In the case of the most memorable interview I ever had, it had nothing to do with the content, everything to do with the circumstances.

For one of my collections of interviews, I had arranged to interview actress-cabaret singer Andrea Marcovicci. I left the venue up to her, and she selected a coffee shop convenient to her home in West Hollywood.

I got there early and looked around, assuring myself that I had arrived first. Because she had suggested meeting at tea time, it was off-hours. There was only one couple in the place, an old man facing in my direction and a woman with her back to me.

Because the room was L-shaped, I took a seat at a table against the wall in the foot of the L where I could keep an eye on the front door. After all, I knew what she looked like and she had no idea how to recognize me.

By 15 minutes after the hour, I had been there for 25 minutes. It wasn't her fault I got there early, but I was getting annoyed. After all, we were meeting here for her convenience, not mine.

Finally, I approached the guy at the cash register and asked him if perhaps Ms. Marcovicci had phoned and left a message. No, she hadn't. But he looked past me and indicated the woman seated with the old guy. "I'm not sure, but I think that might be her."

I turned. I knew Marcovicci from the movies. She had very black hair and wore it long. This woman's hair was barely shoulder length and at least from 40 feet away, it appeared to be auburn.

I decided I had nothing to lose by strolling past their table and making a U-turn so I could see her face.

I did so, but I still wasn't sure. It could have been her, but without the long black hair, I couldn't tell. I risked pausing by the table, where the old man was enjoying his meat loaf, no doubt the early bird special. "Pardon me," I said, "but are you Andrea Marcovicci?"

"Yes."

"I'm here to interview you."

She then turned to the old man and said in a definitely accusatory tone, "So who are you?"

"I'm Burt."

I couldn't help laughing. Apparently the other Burt had been seated, minding his own business, waiting for his meat loaf to arrive when she stopped by and asked him if he was Burt. He said he was and she sat down.

And, so, they had sat for at least half an hour, not exchanging a word. He hadn't asked why she was sitting at his table or why she didn't say a word while he had his supper. On the other hand, she didn't ask why he was eating his meat loaf instead of asking her all the usual questions.

At least I finally understood why she had sat with her back to the door, not bothering to keep an eye out for me. She had found Burt and somehow understood that one Burt is very much like another, except maybe when it comes to meat loaf. I can't stand the stuff.

***

During one Christmas holiday, a friend was invited by Sandy Nimoy to a party she and Leonard were hosting. I was invited to tag along.

By the time we got there, five or six other couples had arrived. Mrs. Nimoy was very good about introducing everyone, which was a good thing because on sight I didn't recognize anyone except her husband. But once I heard their names, I realized that the husbands were all writers or directors.

As the afternoon wore on, the party became increasingly crowded. But by this time, even though she continued to drag late arrivals through the throng, she was simply saying, "George, this is Burt" or "Burt, this is Janet."

As I was merely the guest of a guest, I didn't feel I could ask that she continue to supply last names. I decided the politest way to handle it was to make a point of asking the next person his or her last name while Mrs. Nimoy was still standing there, assuming she would take the hint.

I didn't have long to wait. Two minutes later, she was dragging a woman behind her. "Burt, this is Carol." "Oh, Carol what?" said I. "Carol Burnett," said she.

In my defense, I can only say that although I was a fan and watched her variety show faithfully, she wasn't immediately recognizable because she wasn't smiling and I couldn't see her teeth.

At the time though, by the time she had said "Carol," I recognized her voice. But by then it was too late not to come across like the biggest schnook in town. I had to just stand there and take it as she said "Burnett."

In a way, it wouldn't be all that different if I were at a party in Washington, D.C., and found myself saying "Oh, Barack what?"

A few years later, I had the occasion to interview Carol Burnett. She mentioned her most embarrassing moment had come when she was on one sound stage, rehearsing her show and got word that her all-time favorite actor, Jimmy Stewart, was on an adjoining sound stage.

She immediately ran over to introduce herself and gush about him and his movies.

As she left to go back to work, she backed away from him the way that people do when they're taking their leave from Queen Elizabeth. Not so strange when you realize that Jimmy Stewart constituted Hollywood royalty.

The problem is that a janitor had left a pail on the floor and in stepping backwards, she had stepped in it and got her foot stuck. Rather than stop and remove the pail, she simply clunked off wearing it like a shoe.

After she told me her story, I felt obliged, since it involved her, to remind Carol of my own most embarrassing moment at the Nimoy Christmas party.

When I finished reminding her, she said, "Gee, I don't remember that."

So, apparently, I had needlessly relived my shame.

"Well," I said, "I guess now that's only my second most embarrassing moment."

***

Speaking of Carol Burnett, I had known her sidekick Harvey Korman for several years when, one day, I asked him if he had a million dollars.

When he said, "No way," I was astonished. He had, after all, been making very good money -- or at least I assumed it had been very good money -- first as a regular on Danny Kaye's show and, by the time I put the question to him, for several years on Carol's variety show.

He had no reason to lie, so I simply assumed that between having a family, an agent and Uncle Sam, to support, it was a lot harder to accumulate a million dollars than I had imagined.

Several years later, when I was living in Santa Barbara and had to come to L.A. for meetings with producers or network executives, I would stop and have a drink at the Tail o' the Cock restaurant in Sherman Oaks, waiting for the rush hour traffic to let up on the 101 freeway.

At the time, I hadn't run into Harvey for several years. But I was sitting by myself at the dimly-lit bar nursing my drink, glancing occasionally at my watch, my back to the entrance when I suddenly felt a hand grip my shoulder. It was Harvey Korman. He leaned close, and as if all that time hadn't passed since I'd posed the question, whispered, "Now I have a million dollars."

How he had recognized me from the back, in the gloom, I still have no idea. But I quickly figured out that the money had come pouring in once Burnett's show and its spin-off, "Mama's Family," had gone into syndication.

***

As a rule, I don't approach celebrities unless I'm on assignment or we're working together. But when George Kennedy was celebrating his second marriage in the private room at Chasen's, I was an invited guest. So when I approached Vic Morrow to tell him how much I'd enjoyed his recent performance in a TV movie titled *The Glass House*, in which he'd played the toughest con in a penitentiary, I naturally assumed he would be happy to hear the news. Instead, he turned his back on me. That was bad enough, but I then spotted Mel Torme. I approached to tell him I enjoyed his singing. I had just started to open my mouth when he turned his back on me.

I know I had showered that day and even used a deodorant.

I mean, I was well-aware of the fact that autograph hounds stalked the sidewalk on Beverly Blvd. in front of Chasen's, hoping to corner one of the restaurant's regulars, such as Groucho Marx, Humphrey Bogart, and the Ronald Reagans, who seemed to like the over-rated chili, but I was inside. Obviously, I was there as a friend of our host.

Their behavior made no sense then and it makes no sense now. However, when Vic Morrow died a while later in a freak helicopter accident while shooting a movie, I somehow managed to take it in stride.

***

Of course, I hadn't been working at the Kennedy shindig, so there was no reason, aside from common courtesy, for Morrow and Torme to treat me decently. But when people who had agreed to be interviewed went out of their way to behave like jerks, it made absolutely no sense to me.

Most of them, after all, paid good money to publicists. And

inasmuch as I was generally interviewing them for my column in the Sunday *L.A. Times* (circulation 1.3 million at the time) or *TV Guide* (circulation 14 million), landing me was something of a coup, not because I was so charming and amusing, but because I was a major publicity conduit.

So when George Kennedy introduced me to Robert Mitchum at one of Kennedy's parties and I requested an interview, I wasn't surprised when Mitchum agreed.

However, when I showed up at his office on Sunset Blvd. a few days later, and his secretary led me in, he didn't bother looking up or saying hello. Instead, he sat in his chair reading *Variety* as if he had to commit it to memory before going in front of the cameras.

If it was a test, I'm not sure what kind it might have been. I had already decided he was a jerk and had considered walking out, but for some reason I figured he would chalk it up as a victory. No way was I going to let him win. He would have to get up and leave the office before I did, even if he kept his shnoz stuck in *Variety* for the next three hours.

Finally, I could almost hear him sigh. He put the Hollywood daily aside and we got down to business. He answered all my questions. As interviews with jerks go, it was better than some, worse than others.

***

As a rule, I could be described as a totally guiltless person. It isn't simply that I make every attempt to lead a blameless life, but on those terribly rare occasions when I do slip up the tiniest bit, I tend to find truly excellent reasons why others are actually at fault. Or as I once told my teenage son when he attempted to use me -- I being his alleged role model in this instance, if in no others -- as his reason for having done something he shouldn't have: "Your grandmother was a gold medal winner when it came to instilling guilt, but even she met her match when it came to yours truly. So, don't you even think about it."

However, no matter how much I try to twist and turn, I fear that my days as the Teflon man may have come crashing to a halt. You see, I hold myself partially to blame for Phil Spector's rise and fall. The question I can't avoid asking myself is whether he would now be in prison for murder were it not for me and my good intentions.

As a classmate of Phil's in junior high and high school, I was in attendance the first time he performed in public. The occasion was a school assembly at L.A.'s Fairfax High, back in the mid-50s. Although 60 years have passed, I remember it as if it had happened last week. But that's how it is with major disasters. I'm sure the people who witnessed the crash of the Hindenburg will never forget it, either. And as disasters go, the Hindenburg couldn't hold a candle to Phil's voice.

Five hundred of us sat stunned as Phil strummed his guitar and sang. At least, we assumed he was singing. The idea that anyone with that nasally, Bronx-tinged, wheeze would dare to vocalize outside the confines of his shower or a forest redefined chutzpah for us.

The end of his performance was greeted with absolute silence. After five seconds or so, moved solely by compassion for a fellow human being, my best friend and I started to applaud. Soon, the other students joined in. To our collective horror, this so buoyed Phil's spirits that he did an encore!

Shortly after graduation, Phil, who had seemed destined to be our class's Least Likely to Succeed, began making his mark on the music world, albeit not as a vocalist, but as a composer/record-producer.

When we congregated at the Ambassador Hotel for our 10th reunion, Phil was the one who showed up in a limo he actually owned, along with three bodyguards whose sole function was to ensure that none of us got within ten yards of the maestro.

Is it any wonder that I'm so guilt-stricken? If only I hadn't encouraged Phil that fateful day, I can't help wondering if he might not have become a happy, well-adjusted, accountant, and been spared the drugs, the booze and, finally, the murder conviction.

At the very least, we'd have been spared that really awful encore!

***

In addition to Bob Mitchum, another Hollywood tough guy who gave me a hard time was George C. Scott. At the time Argosy contacted me, Scott had been nominated for an Oscar for his performance in *Patton* and had generated headlines by saying that if he won, he'd refuse to accept.

At the time I was given the assignment, Scott was off in Spain shooting a movie called *The Last Run*, along with his wife Colleen Dewhurst, Tony Musante, and Trish Van Devere.

I was told to stop in New York on my way from L.A. to the location so the editor could give me my marching orders. I don't recall he had much to say except not to waste a lot of time once I got back to L.A. because they needed the copy as soon as possible. However, while I was seated in his office, the door to my left opened and a grizzled-looking guy wearing a hat entered and quickly exited out the door to my right.

He looked familiar from book covers and I asked the editor if that had in fact been William Saroyan. It seemed it was. They had given him an assignment to write about an upcoming fight in which Mohammad Ali would be defending his heavyweight title.

I excused myself and followed Saroyan out the door, which led into an adjoining office. Saroyan had been my favorite writer when I was young, and even though I had since had other favorites, you never forget your first love.

I introduced myself, explained I was heading off to Spain, but wondered if I could interview him once I got back to L.A. and he returned to Fresno. He said he would consider it, but I would first have to send him all my questions.

I explained that I would of course have a few specific questions, but that my way of working was to have a conversation and see where it would lead. He was adamant, so I told him to forget it. I went back to the editor's office to say good-bye.

As it happened, I didn't get back to L.A. quite as quickly as I had expected. It seems that the very day I arrived at my hotel on the Costa del Sol was the same day that Colleen Dewhurst Scott had taken off for NY, her work on the film completed.

It was the same day that Ms. Van Devere took up residence in George C. Scott's bungalow. The cover story was that he had come down with the flu, which, I suppose, meant that Van Devere's duties were those of a nurse.

In any case, shooting shut down for several days, while I waited around, walked on the beach and prayed for his "recovery."

At last the great day arrived. I made my plans to be driven out to the location, only to be told that the director, Richard Fleischer, was still smarting from my summing up his last movie, *Tora! Tora! Tora!* as a "bora, bora, bora" in my *Los Angeles* magazine review of the three-hour turkey.

He told the movie's publicist that if I showed up, he would shut down the production until I left. As a compromise, it was arranged for me to interview Scott in the hotel bar, which would be closed at that hour, before he took off for the location.

I started out by telling him that for the record, I thought Fleischer was a jerk. Most reviewers had dismissed his war epic as second-rate, but it took a real punk to take it out on the reviewer for a small magazine when he would never have pulled this stunt with someone from *Time* or the *New York Times*.

Scott didn't disagree.

I started out by asking him why he had said he wouldn't accept the Oscar if he won the Best Actor competition. He said he didn't believe in competing with other actors. I told him that was baloney.

I pointed out that he had been nominated for two earlier Oscars in the Supporting Actor category, for *The Hustler* and *Anatomy of a Murder*, and he hadn't turned them down. He simply hadn't won.

What's more, he had not only competed for Broadway's Tony awards, but had been a presenter. The only difference between Tonys and Oscars is that everybody knows who wins the Oscars, whereas only a dozen or so people know or care who wins the Tony.

Finally, I pointed out, he had already been in a competition with other actors, which is the competition that really matters -- the initial one for the role.

As great, as I admitted he had been as Patton, it was a tremendous role, and that it's roles that ultimately win Oscars; otherwise, the same five or six people would be nominated every year. I even said that offhand, I could think of several actors who would have been nominated if they had been lucky enough to land *Patton*.

I said that by insisting he wouldn't show up to accept the Oscar, he was merely playing it safe. If he didn't win, he could claim it was because he had announced he wouldn't accept it; but if he did win it, it would mean he was so great that in spite of his threat of boycotting the ceremony, they had no choice but to give it to him.

In the end, I got my story, he got his Oscar, and, best of all, he didn't slug me.

Shortly afterwards, he and Colleen Dewhurst would get a divorce, he and Trish Van Devere would get married, and *The Last Run* would be another flop for Richard Fleischer.

STEVEN HILL WAS JUST TOO JEWISH

When I was in my 20s, my best friend was an orthodox Jew named Howard. Although his father was a successful comedy writer named Irving "Izzy" Elinson, or perhaps because his often-absent boozehound of a father was a successful comedy writer, Howard made a point of insisting he knew nothing about show business. On occasion, he took it to absurd lengths.

For instance, on one occasion, we happened to be at the home of a mutual friend. As we were leaving, Howard noticed the cover of the current *Life* magazine. The cover was upside down and as Howard turned it right-side up, he said "These two look familiar." *These two* were Cary Grant and Audrey Hepburn; *Charade* had just been released. Howard would have been as convincing if the couple on the cover had been Dwight Eisenhower and Richard Nixon.

In any case, that's the background to a phone call I received some years later. Howard was calling, all a-dither. He wanted to know if I had ever heard of an actor named Steven Hill. At least he wasn't asking if I had ever heard of Gary Cooper or Grace Kelly.

The question, though, was why Howard would be asking about a little-known actor. It so happened that I did recognize the name. I had already seen Hill in *The Goddess* and *The Slender Thread*. He hadn't starred in either, but he had been very good. I also was aware that Hill had made his mark portraying Sigmund Freud on Broadway in *A Far Country*.

When I asked Howard what had prompted his question, he said, "Because the guy's been showing up at my shul and showing off!"

My brain promptly began to boggle. How on earth does one show off at an orthodox synagogue? Come dressed like Abe Lincoln? No, that couldn't be it; they all did that.

77

Howard explained: "You know how when I doven (pray), I move my body slowly back and forth?"

Indeed, I did. I had often seen him do so when saying his evening prayers when I'd visit.

"Well, when this character dovens, he moves back and forth like he's running a race. And you know how we orthodox Jews can't eat meat and milk at the same meal?"

Of course I did. After all, I had even been around when we were both 12 years old and how after only one of us had a bar mitzvah when we turned 13, Howard decided to become the only orthodox Jew in a secular household. Howard had insisted, among other things, that his parents buy two sets of dishes and two sets of pots in order that he could live in accordance with the kosher dietary laws.

I even recall the day when, Howard being out of the house, his parents had invited me over to discuss this sudden weird turn of events. Even though I was only 13, I understood what had led up to this. The nearest synagogue to their home happened to be of the orthodox variety, so for the sake of convenience, his parents, figuring one synagogue was the same as another, had him go there.

So it was that for the first time in a great many years, the elderly Hassidic Jews had a young one in their midst and they had made the most of it, showering Howard with a great deal of attention and affection. As I said, his father was often out of the house, drinking with his alcoholic cronies.

Although I was aware of the motivation, I had no idea at the time how deeply the die had been cast. So when his parents asked me what was going on with their son, I confidently replied, like a 13-year-old Dr. Spock: "Don't worry. He's just going through a stage."

I'd been wrong before and I would be wrong again. In fact, when we were at UCLA, if final exams were held on a Friday afternoon, Howard would take an incomplete on religious grounds and retake the exam at some later period because he couldn't risk being in his car at sundown, which marked the advent of Shabbos or Sabbath, when orthodox Jews are forbidden to carry money, turn on lights or go anywhere they couldn't get to by walking.

Getting back to Howard and his problem with Steven Hill, Howard was saying: "You know how we have to have a five-hour separation between eating meat and having a dairy product? Well, according to this guy, nothing less than a seven-hour separation counts! I've never seen such a show-off. He's just so full of himself!"

Since I regularly had meat and dairy at the same meal, I couldn't very well comment, except to say something along the lines of "Some people," which I have found to be the appropriate response on a great many occasions during my life.

Typically, that would have been the end of it. Not this time, though. Not too long after the phone conversation, I was contacted by *TV Guide*. They wanted to know if I would profile Steven Hill, who had recently signed to star in a series set to debut in September. It was called *Mission Impossible*.

I contacted the studio's publicist and he told me to show up the next day at Exposition Park, where the show would be filming some exterior scenes.

I arrived and got to see Hill play a short scene as Dan Briggs, the head of the crime-fighting team.

When they broke for lunch, the cast and crew went one way, Hill the other. They were going to the crafts table, where a catered buffet awaited them. Hill sat down on a long park bench and opened a paper bag. He had provided his own lunch, a hard-boiled egg and a piece of fruit. I sat, lunch-less, holding my pen and steno pad.

I began by asking him about his career. He barely answered. I asked him about *Mission Impossible*. He showed no interest in discussing it. The truth is, I was almost as disinterested as he was. After all, I hadn't even seen the pilot. All the while, I was dying to ask him about all the showing-off at my friend's synagogue. But I was at a loss because I didn't want to embarrass him by even suggesting that he had L.A.'s orthodox Jewish community abuzz with gossip and disdain.

I racked my brain for a question that might open the gate. Finally,

I asked him a question that might not appear too peculiar to an actor: "I was wondering, is Steven Hill your real name?"

At least it diverted his attention away from the hard-boiled egg. He had been leaning forward on the bench. He continued leaning, but he turned his head in my direction. "No," he said, "my name is Solomon Krakovsky."

"Oh," said I, "are you Jewish?"

There was a long pause. Finally, he said, "Yes. Are you?"

"Yes, I am," even though I was aware that the word had different meanings for the two of us. To him, it meant utter devotion to the literal word of the Old Testament and the Torah. To me, it meant having a Russian-Jewish last name, having an affinity for deli cold cuts and rooting for Sandy Koufax.

But, happily, the castle had been breached and, to mix a messy metaphor, the floodgates had exploded.

He was delighted to tell all. He was only too happy to tell me how he had been a secular Jew, seemingly lost in the spiritual wilderness, until he had encountered a charismatic rabbi in Seattle, while he'd been up there shooting *The Slender Thread* with Anne Bancroft and Sidney Poitier.

As a result, he had come to see that up until the scales had fallen from his eyes, he had wasted his life. Acting didn't matter. Money didn't matter. The only thing that really mattered was living a life that expressed his devotion to God.

At one point, he said something to me that I had never thought anyone in real life had ever said to another person. He had apparently warmed up to me once he recognized that I, too, was a member of the tribe, a son of Abraham, although perhaps in my case, more of a step-son or slightly more distant relative. He said, "Have I got a girl for you!"

"Really?" I said, fantasies of some gorgeous starlet prancing in my head.

"Yes, she'd be perfect." He explained that the girl he had in mind was the daughter of the American chess champion, who just happened to be of the orthodox persuasion.

Still, any port in the storm. "Where does she live?"

"In New York."

I pointed out that I lived in California, which would make dating more than slightly out of the question. I suppose in that world, arranged marriages between perfect strangers weren't out of the question, so I hastily popped that bubble by confessing that not only wasn't I orthodox, but I'd never even had a bar mitzvah. He quickly brushed that aside, saying, "It's only traditional to have the ceremony at 13. You can have it at any age."

I told him I'd consider it. I'm still considering it.

We actually spent several hours talking. He was never called back to shoot.

By the time I drove home, the story was pretty much written in my head. But I did go through the motions of interviewing fellow cast members Martin Landau and Barbara Bain, along with the show's creator-producer, Bruce Geller.

The most memorable moment came when I asked Geller if Hill's religiosity created any problems. He did admit that it was slightly inconvenient when they had to conclude his scenes on Friday by mid-afternoon because he had to be home in time to attend services. Oh, and it was a bit of a nuisance when a button had fallen off his jacket during a scene, and when the seamstress rushed forward to sew it back on, and Hill asked her what sort of thread she was using. When she said, "Cotton," he pointed out that the original thread was wool, and he commenced to quote scripture that suggested the mixing of cotton and wool was almost as calamitous as mixing meat and dairy. The seamstress was then forced to track down wool thread before shooting could commence.

When I asked Geller if that wasn't a big headache, he said, "No, it's sort of like working with a diabetic."

I didn't quite see how providing a different meal was the same as stopping production over a spool of thread.

As it turned out, it wasn't the same at all.

When I mailed the piece in, I expected the folks at *TV Guide* to be thrilled. For once, an actor was being profiled who didn't spend the entire article rambling on about what a great show he was working on and how much he adored his fellow cast members.

Instead, *TV Guide* let me know they had no interest in publishing it. As the editor put it, "Nobody is this religious."

I was offered $200 of the usual $500 if I let them have it, to help jump-start a new writer. I opted to take a $100 buy-out, which allowed me to sell it to *Los Angeles* magazine.

By the time *Los Angeles* magazine published the piece, it had been announced that Steven Hill would not be returning for a second season of the hottest show on the air. As usual, creative differences were cited.

In those cases, the presumption is that the actor being tossed out the door had such a wicked cocaine habit that nothing short of six months in a rehab center would get him unhooked or, perhaps, that he had been caught once too often with a 12-year-old boy or girl in his dressing room.

But as the announcement had been made just two days before my article appeared, at least the subscribers to *Los Angeles* magazine knew that Steven Hill wasn't a dope fiend or a pedophile. He simply was *that religious.*

Afterwards, I tried to pick up clues to his whereabouts. I had heard rumors that his marriage had broken up because Hill was demanding that their two sons study to be rabbis and their two daughters be raised to be worthy of being married to rabbis.

It was a bridge too far for his secular wife and she divorced him.

I then heard through a friend whose parents resided in the orthodox Jewish community about an hour north of New York City in Rockland County that Hill had moved there.

For years, I heard nothing more. Then, after a long absence during which he had apparently gone into the real estate business, he began to appear in movies shot in New York, among them *Running on Empty*, *Brighton Beach Memoirs*, and *Garbo Talks*.

As I heard it, every morning a bus leaves Rockland with a load of orthodox Jews who work in New York City, generally in the diamond district. At night, it transports them back.

As an actor, he was as believable as ever. Just a bit balder and more grizzled.

Then, he began a 10-year stint as D.A. Adam Schiff on *Law & Order*.

When I last checked, Steven Hill was 94-years-old. He had married for a second time in 1967 and had another five children.

As in all matters, Hill had taken to heart God's injunction to go forth and multiply. He had never won an Oscar, an Emmy, or a Tony. But with nine children to his credit, I'm sure he feels he's done right in the eyes of his own personal director.

THE GREAT ONE

The plan was for me to have lunch with Jackie Gleason at the Polo Lounge on Friday, and then follow him up to Burlingame, an upscale suburb of San Francisco, on Monday. Burlingame was where Gleason was set to begin shooting an Otto Preminger movie titled *Skidoo*.

Lunch, as was often the case in those bygone days, was a boozy one. Of course Gleason was notorious for his alcohol consumption, and I had decided to impress him by matching him drink for drink. Fat chance. After two drinks, he began lapping me and I knew better than to challenge him. If I had drunk as much as Gleason did in those three hours, they would have taken me directly to Forest Lawn. He, on the other hand, might as well have been drinking orange juice.

In fact, when he finally got up to empty his bladder, I expected him to fall on his face. Instead, he pranced off as if his nickname were "Mr. Twinkletoes" instead of "The Great One."

A couple of things I recall his mentioning was that he had taken the train out from Florida to California because he was afraid of flying, and that the reason he had signed up to do what promised to be a lousy movie was because of the deal.

The deal, he patiently explained, was the only way to judge talent. "For instance," he said, "Paul Newman and Robert Redford are both great. The only way to tell which one is greater is by comparing their last deals."

He went on to say that when he was approached to do *Take Me Along* on Broadway, he had no burning desire to appear on stage. But he asked the producers who had been paid the most to do a musical and was told that Alfred Drake had been paid $5,000-a-week to do *Kismet*. So Gleason asked for $5,050, and when the producers agreed, he signed on for a year.

In the case of *Skidoo*, he said the selling point was that he would

85

share in the gross, not the usual net, which in Hollywood seemed to vanish like the morning dew.

As we took our leave, Gleason signed the tab and shared a secret with me. "I never fill in the tip amount. I always let the waiter or waitress do it."

When I asked why, he said, "If I filled it in, no matter how generous I was, they'd call me a cheapskate. This way, I let them write in whatever they think is fair. I'm sure I've saved thousands of dollars over the years."

On Monday, I traveled up to Burlingame. By this time, I was one of the 10 million people on earth that Gleason called "Pal." It was easier than trying to remember names.

I discovered that as much as Gleason liked his booze, when there was night shooting, he never took his first drink of the day until he had finished working.

We fell into a pattern where I would watch the shoot and then return to the motel to drink and resume our interview. One evening, he looked at me and said, "Pal, are you able to drink every day?"

It seemed an odd question, but I said, "I suppose I could, but I don't."

"You're lucky. If I drank every day, I'd be a dead man. I only drink every other day."

I soon came to discover how true that was. One morning after we had been drinking the night before, I passed him in the corridor of the motel and his eyelids were drooping so low, he didn't even see me. The surprise is that he didn't walk into a wall.

One day, Harry Nilsson, the young singer-composer who was scoring *Skidoo*, asked me if I would introduce him to Gleason. Nilsson would go on to have his greatest success singing someone else's song, "Everybody's Talkin' (At Me)" made famous when it was used extensively in *Midnight Cowboy*. He was a nice young guy I'd gotten to know while hanging around the set. It turned out he was a great fan of the instrumental albums Gleason had composed and conducted.

I told Harry to show up that night in the motel bar after Gleason and I returned from the location. I explained that the best time to meet Gleason was after he'd had a couple of shots and a chance to unwind after working. I told him to wait until I signaled him to come over.

That night, there were three of us in the booth, Jackie, myself, and Jackie's girlfriend, Marilyn Taylor, whom Jackie always called "Honey." At the time, I assumed that was her actual name, so I, too, called her "Honey." Marilyn, by the way, was the sister of choreographer June Taylor. The June Taylor Dancers appeared regularly on Gleason's variety show.

Gleason seemed to be in a friendly mood, so after he'd had his requisite shots, I signaled Nilsson that it was time to be introduced. Resembling a very happy puppy, he hurried over. I introduced him to Gleason, letting Jackie know that Harry was the young man who was going to score the movie and making a point of letting Gleason know that he loved Gleason's music.

The transition was so sudden that you would have thought I had told Gleason that Harry thought he was a musical hack, a lousy comic and oh, by the way, drank too much. Gleason got that morning-after look, with the hooded eyelids lowered to half-mast, and snarled: "You're a punk. You think you have talent? I wrote my theme song 'Melancholy Serenade' in five minutes. What the hell have you ever done?"

I don't know who was more shocked, Harry Nilsson or me. Harry might have blinked back tears once or twice before turning and rushing off.

When I looked back at Gleason, it was as if the past 20 seconds had never occurred. He was smiling and chatting with Honey. It was such a surreal moment, I found myself wondering if I had had a hallucination. But Harry was gone, so I knew I hadn't dreamed it.

I was angry, feeling that I had been responsible for sucker-punching the kid. When I asked Gleason why he had said those things, the best he could come up with was that Nilsson was a punk. It made no sense, except that Nilsson, as was typical at the time, wore his hair fairly long.

I apologized to Harry the next morning, but I still felt that Gleason had betrayed me, and by this time I knew better than to blame it on the booze. The man just had a very nasty side to him, and perhaps the booze was the potion that allowed him to transform himself from Dr. Jekyll to Mr. Hyde and back again, as his mood dictated.

The next evening's shoot took place in a rented mansion. It provided me with the opportunity to see another egotist give vent to his own Mr. Hyde.

In the scene, for purposes of the plot, a phony fire had to be produced. It was to be carried off by having a member of the crew perched beneath the staircase with a bellows. It was his job to provide smoke for the camera. But no matter how much smoke or how little, director Otto Preminger wasn't satisfied. He just kept hollering at the poor guy in front of all of us.

When Preminger wasn't hollering at him, he was shouting at character actor Arnold Stang. He didn't care for the way that Stang was reading his lines, but instead of telling him what he wanted, Preminger's direction consisted of shouting insults at him.

Even though the cast was filled with "names," including Carol Channing, Frankie Avalon, Frank Gorshin, Peter Lawford, Burgess Meredith, George Raft, Cesar Romero, Mickey Rooney, Groucho Marx and, of course, Jackie Gleason, I noticed that Preminger never yelled at any of them.

When I called this to Gleason's attention, he just laughed. "Otto knows if he raised his voice to me, I'm on the train, headed back to Florida."

The next day, I was having lunch with the company. I was seated next to Gleason; Preminger was seated at the picnic table directly across from me. I could barely stand to look at him. Even though I knew he was Jewish, he looked exactly like the Nazi commandant he had portrayed in Billy Wilder's *Stalag 17*.

At one point, two men in suits approached Preminger, and the three of them walked about twenty feet away. They had a brief conversation. After which, the two strangers left and Preminger came back to the table.

Although I had paid scant attention to the three of them and couldn't possibly have heard what they were talking about, Preminger turned a cold eye on me that required only a monocle to make it even more menacing, and said, "You won't write about this."

"About what?"

"About the fact that Bobby Kennedy's people asked me for an endorsement. I don't want it to look like they had to ask."

Bobby Kennedy was campaigning for the presidency that year, but I didn't care if they had to ask for Preminger's endorsement or if he had simply volunteered his name and money. What was important was that Preminger cared.

Although there was no reason for the episode to appear in a lengthy profile of Gleason, the opportunity was simply too good to pass up.

"I'll think about it," I told Preminger.

"You won't write about it!" he shouted, the spittle flying out of his nasty little mouth.

"I don't work for you. You don't get to tell me what to write. However, I am willing to make a deal."

"What kind of deal?"

"I won't write about it, but in return you won't scream at anyone today."

"What are you talking about?"

"When you resume shooting, you will speak quietly to the crew and the actors. No more shouting."

"But," he actually said, "they like it when I shout."

"No, they don't. But even if for some strange reason they did, I don't, and I'm the one offering you the deal."

He stared at me. Finally, he stuck his hand out.

"Okay, it's a deal." We shook. He kept his word.

A few days later, I left. For the most part, I had enjoyed my time with Gleason. But I couldn't get the image of Harry Nilsson looking like he was about to cry out of my head.

Gleason was a great many things -- actor, comedian, composer, pool shark, boozer extraordinaire -- but one thing that he wasn't was The Greatest.

SNAPSHOTS III

Back before there were answering machines, people would pay for an answering service. If you weren't home, one of the ladies at the service would take the call and write down the message. When you'd return home, you'd call the service number and collect your messages.

One afternoon, I called in as usual and was told I had one message. The lady told me that Sonny Tufts had phoned and left a number.

I knew who Tufts was, but I had never met him and I couldn't imagine why he would have called me. But by this time, Johnny Carson had taken to making jokes that would include Tufts' name, so I assumed a friend was pranking me.

Still, I didn't recognize the number, and when I dialed it the voice at the other end identified himself as the pool guy at the Beverly Hills Hotel. I asked to speak to Sonny Tufts, and was told he'd been there, but had left. I was also told that he was generally around at lunch time.

The next day I phoned and reached him. I introduced myself and asked why he had called. He said he read me regularly in the Sunday edition of the *L.A. Times* and just wanted to let me know how much he enjoyed my column.

I, in turn, asked if I could interview him. He agreed and we made a lunch date.

When he said lunch, he clearly meant booze. It was a very pleasant and amusing few hours. I wasn't surprised that he had edited the humor magazine in college. He was very funny, and usually at his own expense.

I discovered that his real name was Bowen Charlton Tufts III. "Sonny" had been his family nickname.

His was a prominent banking family and that among its philanthropic efforts had been the creation of Tufts University.

As Sonny told it, the plan was for him to follow in the footsteps of previous generations, but he bugged out to study opera. By doing so, he assured me, generations of widows and orphans had not been made insolvent.

When an opera career didn't exactly pan out, Tufts turned his attention to Broadway. That, in turn, led to a contract with Paramount. As luck would have it, his first movie, *So Proudly We Hail*, was a smash hit starring Claudette Colbert, Veronica Lake, and Paulette Goddard. In his debut, Sonny appeared as Goddard's love interest.

Because Sonny was tall, blond, and muscular, he was what the movies used to promote as beefcake, the male equivalent of cheesecake. As soon as the movie was released, 2,000 fan letters-a-week began arriving at Paramount.

With World War II raging and most of the town's leading men in uniform, Tufts, who was 4F because of an old football injury, quickly found himself in one movie after another.

In evaluating his acting ability, Tufts was the same good-natured lug off the screen as on. In his own words, he was a lousy actor, "But if Paramount was willing to pay me $5,000-a-week, I was happy to accept it."

I asked him if he was aware of the fact that the foremost movie critic at the time, James Agee, disagreed with his self-evaluation. Tufts had never even heard of Agee, who reviewed movies for both *Time* magazine and the *Nation*. I, being a movie critic at the time, had just finished reading a collection of Agee's reviews.

Agee was definitely a fan, often dismissing Tufts' movies as trifles, but going on to admonish Paramount for wasting what Agee considered a uniquely American talent. Tufts could barely believe his ears.

After all, in what has been dismissed as something of an urban legend, but which Sonny swore actually happened, Joseph Cotton had just finished acting in a radio drama when he was handed a sheet on which he was supposed to plug the following week's episode. The copy about the next guest star was so gushing, you would have expected him to be someone of the stature of Robert Donat, Laurence Olivier, or Paul Muni. But when Cotton got to the actor's name, he was so startled, he said: "SONNY TUFTS?!" into a live mic.

According to Tufts, Joseph Cotton was so embarrassed, he phoned Sonny the next day to apologize. But Tufts told him to forget it. He thought it was funny.

In any case, I promised to send Tufts a copy of Agee's book. But when I got home, I decided that instead of mailing it, once the interview was printed, I would invite Tufts to lunch and hand him the book.

Because my articles appeared in the Sunday supplement of the *Times*, *WEST* magazine, I had to have my copy in two or three weeks ahead of publication.

At the time, I was also writing book reviews for the paper. So it was that late one Friday evening, I was working on a review. It was the wee hours of Saturday morning before I finished. Because it had to be at the *Times* Monday morning, I knew if I sent it directly from the post office, it would save me a trip downtown.

By the time I got home, the Saturday paper had arrived. Because I was so wide awake, I decided to read the *Times* before going to bed.

There, on the front page of the second section was a picture of Sonny Tufts. He had died at the age of 58. My first reaction was that it couldn't possibly be true. I had seen him just a couple of weeks before and he looked perfectly healthy, but, then, I hadn't seen his liver. The paper reported that he'd died of pneumonia.

My second reaction was that my tongue-in-cheek interview was going to appear the next day. Would people realize that I had written it weeks earlier? Or would they simply assume I had written the most tasteless obituary in journalistic history?

On Monday, my editor called to let me know that Sonny's sister had phoned to say she loved Sonny's send-off and that she was sure that Sonny would have loved it, too.

My third reaction was that I shouldn't have waited. I should have sent Sonny James Agee's book of film criticism when I first thought of it.

The lesson I was taught is that if you ever decide to do something nice for someone, go ahead and do it. Don't dawdle because you just never know how long either of you will be around.

***

I don't have a great deal to say about meeting Fred Astaire, except that I felt as if I were in the presence of someone I had only read about in a book. By the time I found myself seated in his sunny den, he had already hung up his dancing shoes, but he was still the same epitome of style and class he had been on the screen. He continued to forswear belts, employing his trademark scarf to hold up his grey flannel trousers.

He still looked as sleek and svelte as a greyhound, so he either exercised as much as he had when he would rehearse a dance number eight hours-a-day for weeks at a time or he had the metabolism of a humming bird.

The moment I remember best came after I had asked him his opinion of the current dance crazes, none of which involved holding your partner or moving around the room to a recognizable melody.

In response, he waved his hand dismissively, with a single gesture displaying his contempt for all the dances that called for keeping one's feet stationery while moving the rest of your body as spasmodically as possible.

He slid off his barstool to show me what he meant, but, of course, when Fred Astaire made an attempt to look gawky and clumsy, it came off looking, to use one of his favorite words, swell.

He stopped after a few seconds, sat back on his barstool and said, "With their hair swinging around, women can look all right doing it, but men just look dumb."

Not if they happen to be Fred Astaire.

***

One day, a producer and I paid a visit to Darren McGavin. McGavin had been a reliable character actor for many years, most notably as Louis, the drug pusher in *Man with a Golden Arm*, but he had become a bigger name as the result of playing the intrepid reporter on TV's *Kolchak: The Night Stalker* and would later go on to gain immortality as the harassed father in *Christmas Story*.

We showed up at McGavin's office in hopes of enticing him to commit to a TV series. I believe it was a comedy-western. But I'm not sure after all this time if he even gave us a chance to go into our spiel.

Something that was said after "Hello" set him off. Although neither of us had ever met him and neither of us had suggested we were licensed to practice psychiatry in the state of California, he began telling us how much he hated his brother.

Perhaps we had suggested he might have a brother in the series or perhaps he was merely as crazy as a horse high on locoweed. In any case, without the slightest bit of prompting, he told us that his "brother" was the result of his father's philandering. He had no idea who the other woman was; he only knew that the boy was being raised by his own parents and that this "love child," as McGavin called him, was clearly his father's favorite.

As he told us this, McGavin was clearly in the grip of an anger that had lasted through the years, and had probably only increased with the passage of time.

When he finished his recital, he calmed down and politely informed us that he wasn't interested in our series.

To this day, I have no idea if he even knew what our series involved. But, to be honest, by the time we left, we were in such a state of shock and confusion, I'm not sure we did either.

***

When I was working at Talent Associates, I became friendly with a couple of comedy writer-producers named Arne Sultan and Chris Hayward. One of the perks of befriending them was that I would be invited to the annual Christmas bash held in the wine cellar of Scandia's, a beautiful restaurant that marked the western end of the Sunset Strip. Scandia's was always first-rate and it went all out for the holidays. The dining room was beautifully decorated and sported an enormous Christmas tree. A troupe of Christmas carolers were always on hand to help us pretend we were enjoying a white Christmas in spite of the temperature typically being in the mid-70s.

The group into which I was initiated was limited to 12, that being how many chairs would fit around the wooden table that took up most of the space in the wine cellar. Over the next several years, the core included Sultan, Hayward, me, D.J. Gary Owens, who would always have to rush off a little early to make it to his radio show in Hollywood, and Bob Wallerstein, who was the lawyer for a few of us. Depending on their work schedule and whether they were in town, we might be joined by Ed Asner, Barney Phillips, David Wayne, and Grant Tinker.

With the passage of time I've forgotten a few of the others in the group. But the one I remember best was the fellow who arranged these festive get-togethers, Collier Young, who would take the occasion every year to break out the lederhosen, which seemed, for some odd reason, to symbolize Christmas for him.

As a young man, Collier had served as a secretary for the great, now nearly forgotten, novelist, Booth Tarkington. Although at the height of his fame, Tarkington may have been best known for his boyhood tales of life in Indiana revolving around the adventures of Penrod and his friend Sam, his best work, *Alice Adams* and *The Magnificent Ambersons*, are among the greatest novels ever written. Both won Pulitzer Prizes, and it is shameful that he is no longer read and is generally dismissed by the critics as "a regionalist," whereas Mark Twain and William Faulkner, whose best books were also regional in nature, sit atop the pantheon of American authors.

At the time of the Christmas lunches, Collier Young was enjoying great success as the creator and producer of the Raymond Burr TV series, *Ironside*. But, I always thought that his greatest achievement wasn't in entertainment, but in the world of diplomacy.

96

As a diplomat, Young was truly in a league of his own. To begin with, he was not only married four times, but maintained cordial relations with all of his ex-wives. What's more, two of them were movie stars named Ida Lupino and Joan Fontaine. In fact, in her autobiography, Ms. Fontaine had little good to say about her sister Olivia De Havilland or anyone else she had ever known or worked with, but wrote glowingly about Collie.

However, not only did this magician somehow manage to remain on friendly terms after the seemingly inevitable divorce, but he produced a TV series, *Mr. Adams and Eve*, starring Lupino and her next husband, Howard Duff.

That was impressive, but it was only his opening act, for not only did he go on to produce several of the movies Ms. Lupino would later direct, but on one of them, *The Bigamist*, he somehow managed to wrangle Joan Fontaine into co-starring with Lupino and then, for good measure, included a former mother-in-law in the cast! "No Guts, No Glory" could have been his own personal motto.

***

Arnold Lipsman was my favorite flack, mainly because he was funny and had a clear-eyed view of what he did for a living and an equally honest view of those for whom he labored, a list that included Robin Williams, Billy Crystal, Sammy Davis, along with the team of Steve Lawrence and his wife Eydie Gorme.

Probably Lipsman's least favorite time of year was when the annual *Comic Relief* telethon rolled around. Because two of his PR clients, Billy Crystal and Robin Williams, were involved in hosting the event along with Whoopi Goldberg, and Lipsman was the target of their complaints. As he would tell me, after the first couple of years, Billy Crystal would regularly whine about being roped in by the other two, begging Arnold to find an honorable way to be released from the commitment. He also felt at a distinct disadvantage because whereas he was accustomed to working off a script, Williams preferred winging it.

The other complaint Lipsman received on a regular basis would come his way from Robin Williams, who was forever griping that whenever a dinner check would arrive, Crystal would either be in the men's room or discovering that he'd left his wallet at home.

Williams insisted it was Arnold's job to let Crystal know that he had developed a reputation as a cheapskate. Arnold would suggest it was really Robin's responsibility as Billy's friend, whereas it would only become his own if the news went viral and he then had to formulate a public relations campaign to counteract the negative publicity.

So far as I know, neither of them ever said a word about it to Crystal, who, as a result, has been able to save hundreds of thousands of dollars over the years by employing his version of alligator arms every time a restaurant check has landed on the table.

***

Although Oscar and June Levant didn't throw a lot of parties, they generally had seven or eight couples over for Christmas dinner.

The year I recall best, Cornel Wilde and his actress wife, Jean Wallace, were among the guests. Wilde and I got along splendidly, mainly, I imagine, because I'd given the movie he'd produced, directed, and starred in, *The Naked Prey*, a rave review.

When Wilde and I spoke about the movie that had put him on the map some 25 years earlier, *A Song to Remember*, in which his performance as Chopin had garnered him his only Oscar nomination, he shared his one disappointment about the movie. That was having to work with Paul Muni, whom Wilde described as the rudest and most arrogant actor in Hollywood. What angered him the most was that whenever it came time to reverse the camera angle and do Wilde's close-ups, Muni would retire to his dressing room and have the script girl feed Wilde his lines.

But, as it happened, the person I wound up talking to the most was the English suspense novelist, Eric Ambler, whose works included *The Mask of Dimitrios*, *The Light of Day*, and *Journey into Fear*.

Somehow, fueled no doubt by liquor, we got into a heated exchange about New York City, of all things. Whereas I felt that it was unfortunate that New York had become the cultural center of America, Ambler contended it was not only inevitable, but a very good thing.

I argued that it might make sense that London and Paris would serve that role, both being the political centers as well as, more or less, the geographic centers, of the two nations, but that it made far less sense in the case of New York.

After all, Washington, D.C., was the political hub and either Chicago or St. Louis might be regarded as the nation's geographical center. Thanks to Wall Street, New York could be considered the financial hub, but that was a lousy reason for its being the cultural arbiter of the entire nation.

I pointed out that the result was that New York felt itself not only closer to London than it did to Los Angeles, although it was a thousand miles farther away, but that its critics felt it appropriate, if not downright imperative, to dismiss such writers as Willa Cather, William Saroyan, Carson McCullers, John Steinbeck, Robinson Jeffers, Ross Lockridge, Nelson Algren, Erskine Caldwell, Flannery O'Connor, Sherwood Anderson, and the aforementioned Booth Tarkington, as regional. The only reason that people like Raymond Chandler, Ross MacDonald, Dashiell Hammett, and John MacDonald weren't dismissed in similar fashion is because it was easier to demean their talents by referring to them as mystery writers, just as it was more convenient to dismiss Zane Gray, Max Brand, and Louis L'Amour, as hacks dedicated to churning out mere westerns.

As for the southern Tennessee Williams and the mid-western William Inge, the only thing preventing them from suffering a similar fate was that their work was staged on Broadway, and so it was New York critics who had first crack at bestowing benedictions on their work. Even so, they were far more respectful to Arthur Miller, who, aside from *Death of a Salesman*, was basically a left-wing scold, a man best-suited to write heavy-handed essays about political matters for *The Atlantic* or *The Nation*.

At the same time, if a writer set all his work in Brooklyn, the Bronx, Queens or, best of all, Manhattan, he was regarded in his or her full glory as a truly American writer.

It also helps explain why New York continues to hold Hollywood in contempt, just as it did in the 30s and 40s. It has never gotten beyond despising the movies and, later, TV, for responding to the siren call of California's weather. It was why they labeled writers, directors, actors, and composers, sell-outs if they went west to ply their trades. So it was that while Hollywood was turning out the likes of *Mutiny on the Bounty*, *My Favorite Wife*, *It's a Wonderful Life*, *Destry Rides Again*, *Gone with the Wind*, *The Wizard of Oz*, *The Best Years of Our Lives*, *Citizen Kane*, and Astaire & Rogers musicals, in New York the critics continued insisting that the fat and fatuous novels of Theodore Dreiser and the pretentious stage offerings of Eugene O'Neill were works of genius.

Although I'm convinced that I won the fight on points, even if I wasn't able to knock him out, Ambler seemed equally convinced that he had won, although I don't recall his making any convincing arguments in defense of his position.

It's true that after dinner, Cornel Wilde let me know he agreed with me. But I'm enough of a realist to understand that may not have been because I had actually persuaded him, but because I may have gone slightly overboard in my review of *The Naked Prey*.

***

I was always surprised that most of the world seemed shocked to learn only after he had contracted AIDS that Rock Hudson was gay. It had always seemed obvious to me. Of course, living in L.A., as we both did, the rumors had long abounded about his having "married" actor-singer Jim Nabors and L.A. Rams quarterback Roman Gabriel at a small church in the San Fernando Valley. But so far as I'd been concerned, the real tip-off was his eyes. Particularly in love scenes, even those involving his friend, Doris Day, they had always struck me as cold, exposing the self-contempt he clearly felt for having to conceal his sexual identity. The need to protect his screen image even extended to his having to go through an actual marriage ceremony with his agent's secretary.

I only got to meet him when I finally wrote a couple of scripts for *McMillan & Wife*. He even ad-libbed my name in one of the episodes when he was trying to recall some character's name.

When I went to his hillside home in Beverly Hills to conduct an interview, it was reminiscent of visiting Mae West's apartment, not because it had all white walls and white carpeting, but because I had never seen so many young men with muscles in one place.

Hudson was cooperative, as he always was with the press, but I got the distinct impression that he was almost as anxious for me to leave as I was to depart. It wasn't that I felt I had interrupted a pool party, but that it was going to be delayed until I left.

***

Although I had been a fan of his, especially his arrangement of "Begin the Beguine," meeting Artie Shaw (born Arthur Jacob Arshawsky) was something of a letdown. Shortly after I moved to Santa Barbara, I was invited by a friend to attend a lunch at the beachside Miramar Hotel, where every month 12 or 15 local writers, musicians, and cartoonists, would gather.

The first month I was a guest, someone else invited Artie Shaw. I was introduced to him as a writer for *M*A*S*H*. His response was "I never watch TV." Then he turned and walked away.

In time, I was to learn that Shaw considered himself a genius, a true renaissance man. His basis for this was that he shot skeet; had once written a 2,000-page unpublished and unpublishable novel; his music, of course; and, I suppose, the fact that he had been married to eight women.

When he finally gave up playing the clarinet, he explained that he had taken the instrument as far as it could go, and with the advance of age he could no longer meet his own perfectionist standards. And when he gave up music altogether, he again referred to his own impossible standards, and said that, unlike, say, Irving Berlin, he couldn't bear to just keep repeating himself musically.

Yes, the ego that walked like a man actually placed himself above the genius who had written the words and music for "Alexander's Ragtime Band," "Cheek to Cheek," "Isn't This a Lovely Day," "Easter Parade," "There's No Business Like Show Business," the entire scores of *Call Me Madam* and *Annie Get Your Gun* and, oh yeah, "God Bless America."

Which makes Shaw's eight marriages even harder to figure out. After his first two marriages to the anonymous likes of Jane Cairns and Margaret Allen, he proceeded to marry actresses Lana Turner; Doris Dowling; Ava Gardner; Evelyn Keyes; Kathleen Winsor, best-selling author of *Forever Amber*, and Betty Kern, the daughter of composer Jerome Kern. The first seven marriages lasted, on average, one and a half years. Somehow, he managed to remain married to Ms. Keyes for 28 years, before that one, too, ended in the divorce court.

Hard to imagine how someone who regarded himself as a perfectionist who couldn't bear repeating himself, repeatedly strolled down the marriage aisle for the better part of 40 years.

In each case, the reason for the divorce was that Shaw was verbally abusive. That was easy to believe because the next time I laid eyes on him was about 10 years later when he and another guy were seated at a nearby table in an Italian restaurant, in West L.A.

On that occasion, he never stopped talking about Ava Gardner. That is to say he never stopped talking about how incredibly stupid she was.

Never having met the lady, I can't comment about her intelligence. But at least she was smart enough to dump the arrogant bully in less than a year.

***

Perhaps it was because the assignment from *Holiday* magazine was to profile English movie director Richard Lester, who had just shot *A Funny Thing Happened on the Way to the Forum*, and not the show's composer-lyricist, Stephen Sondheim, that Sondheim was seemingly disinterested in a British drawing room sort of way; however, I had been warned by one of his associates that it was his typical pose, unless he was in hot pursuit of a Broadway chorus boy.

Sondheim did loosen up enough to confess that he felt as if he had sold his soul in agreeing to stifle his own musical talents by serving as Leonard Bernstein's lyricist on *West Side Story* and Jule Styne's on *Gypsy*.

It was only years later that I discovered that the neighbor living in the adjoining New York brownstone was Katherine Hepburn. If I had known, I would have at least knocked on her door and told her I wished she had won at least a couple of her Oscars for comedy.

I came away from my interlude with Sondheim wondering how much it bothered him that, aside from "Send in the Clowns," the only real hits in his career had come about as the result of collaborating with Bernstein and Styne.

I was also left wondering if the all-white jigsaw puzzle he had prominently displayed in his living room had come that way or whether he had, in fact, put it together on his own. I had thought about asking him, but I suspected he was prepared to lie.

***

Because we had a mutual friend who played tennis, I would occasionally encounter Ed Kleban on the tennis courts. At the time, he was working for Columbia Records, producing albums for artists as disparate as Igor Stravinsky and Percy Faith.

When I stopped seeing Ed on the courts, I didn't spend a lot of time wondering where he was. Then, one night, while watching the

Tony Awards on TV, I suddenly heard his name called out and there he was hustling up the aisle with Marvin Hamlisch to collect his Tony as the lyricist for *A Chorus Line*.

At least now I knew where he had gone, even if I hadn't the slightest clue how it had happened. That had to wait for a year or so, until *A Chorus Line* came to L.A. and the publicity director for the Century City Theatre contacted me, wondering if I'd be interested in interviewing Kleban. I was.

By the time we got together, Kleban had not only won a Tony, but along with his four collaborators on the show, had picked up a Pulitzer Prize. I learned during our lunch that he had always wanted to be creatively involved in the theater, but that it had taken an act of sheer will to walk away from his $100,000-a-year salary in order to go back to New York and enroll in the prestigious Lehman Engel Musical Theater Workshop.

He had worked as a lyricist for a few New York revues. But it was his good fortune that after a number of other potential lyricists, apparently including Sondheim, had begged off because of their busy schedules, he had finally been approached to work on *A Chorus Line*.

He recalled that the day after the show had opened to the sort of reviews that guaranteed a very long and prosperous run, he and Hamlisch had exited the theater through the alley and when they came out to the street, they saw that the line of people waiting to buy tickets stretched seemingly to the horizon.

"Soak it in," Hamlisch advised him. "This is probably going to be the greatest day of our lives."

Kleban confessed that he and his collaborator had had to beg the creator/producer/director of the show, Michael Bennett, to allow them to keep the song "What I Did for Love" in the show. They knew it was their one shot at a hit, which was exactly why Bennett didn't want it. He felt that the integrity of the show, perhaps one might say its soul, would be irreparably sullied, if, like every other Broadway musical it lived or died on its hit tunes.

Fortunately, Bennett finally caved in to their pleas and allowed the show to have its creative aspirations slightly compromised.

I was reminded that on other occasions, Harold Arlen and Yip Harburg had had to beg Louis B. Meyer to let them keep "Over the Rainbow" in *The Wizard of Oz* and Arlen and Ira Gershwin had had to chase Sid Luft down on a golf course before they could persuade the husband/producer of Judy Garland's *A Star is Born* to keep "The Man That Got Away" in the final cut. But that's because Meyer and Luft had tin ears, not because they cared about creative aspirations.

Without Arlen, Harburg, and Gershwin's powers of persuasion, Garland's concert repertoire would have been limited to "The Trolley Song" and "We're Off to See the Wizard."

The big surprise of the interview with Kleban came when he confessed he'd love to compose theme songs for TV sitcoms and wondered if I had an in. Unfortunately, I didn't. Thus, he was doomed to be satisfied with a Tony, a Pulitzer, and having played a major role in creating the sixth longest-running musical in Broadway history.

In fact, by the time *A Chorus Line* ended its run in 1990, it had out-lasted Kleban, who had died of throat cancer two years earlier, at the age of 48.

WC FIELDS' OWN LITTLE CHICKADEE

A photographer for the *L.A. Times* had been driving around town on the search for classic cars, which he intended to highlight in a pictorial essay for the paper. When he found that a 1938 Cadillac he had spotted outside a small bungalow in Hollywood belonged to Carlotta Monti and that the car had been given to her by W.C. Fields, he contacted the newspaper's managing editor, who then informed me.

I met Carlotta and we became good friends. At the time, she was in her mid-60s and working nights at Technicolor. Fields had already been dead for about 25 years.

We started out talking about the car. It seems that even though she had lived with Fields for 14 years, when he died, he didn't mention her in his will. But there had been an envelope in his safe that contained $50,000. Written on the envelope in his handwriting was "Carlotta Monti." But when it was contested by Fields' son, the court decided that the money belonged to the family because he hadn't written "*For* Carlotta Monti."

He did leave her his car, which had been in storage for years, but she had to fight for it in court and she had to pay the storage fees before she could take possession.

The reverse of most people, Carlotta liked Fields, but she never thought he or his movies were funny. "For some reason, people seemed to think that just because he talked out of the side of his mouth," she'd say, talking out of the side of her mouth and doing a pretty fair impersonation, "people thought he was hilarious."

The two met when she was doing bit parts in movies, usually as an exotic temptress. She reported that he was just about as acerbic off-camera as on, but that so long as she didn't take him seriously, they got along fine.

Carlotta said that the only time she saw Fields out of character was the day in 1941 that C.B. DeMille's two-year-old grandson, the son of Anthony Quinn and Katherine DeMille, wandered across DeMille Drive and onto his property, where he toppled into a pond and drowned.

Monti said she had never seen Fields in such anguish. He had the pond cemented over the next day.

At the time that I met and interviewed Carlotta, I was living in a small house near the top of a Hollywood hill. It was there that she picked me up a few days later. She had decided to get her nephew to chauffeur us around in the Cadillac, while she pointed out the various haunts where she had lived with Fields.

Now as a rule, I would record my interviews in a steno notebook, using a form of shorthand I had come up with. It was sufficient to my needs. One of the nice things about it was that if I started to fall behind, I could catch up when the subject was telling me stuff I knew I wouldn't be using. Best of all, so far as they knew, I found everything they said so fascinating, I wanted to be sure to capture every single word.

However, my managing editor, Jim Bellows, who had once overseen the *New York Herald-Tribune*, and never let anyone forget it, was always going on about the likes of Tom Wolfe, Jimmy Breslin and Gail Sheehy, and insisting that, like them, I should use a tape recorder.

I didn't cotton to the notion. I figured that because I never trusted mechanical devices, I would never stop worrying that it wasn't working right. Also, it would mean I would have to listen to the entire interview, whereas when I transcribed it in my notebook, I could edit, as I said, as I went along.

But, I didn't want my editor to think I was so out of touch, I was still writing with a quill. So, for the first time ever, I used the device to record our conversation as she showed me the two houses where they had lived, the one on DeMille Drive, another above Beverly Hills close to John Barrymore's place, and a park where they would often picnic.

By the time they dropped me off, I had used up three tapes.

Because I dreaded the notion of transcribing all that material, I let the tapes sit on the top of my stereo for a few days. In the meantime, with the Academy Awards coming up, I had made my bets with a friend on the eventual winners. I had copied down our choices on a paper napkin. I also left that next to the tapes. I only mention this because that same week, my house was burgled.

When the cops asked me if I suspected anyone, I refrained from mentioning the Three Stooges. It was almost embarrassing to mention what they had carted off. The entire list consisted of two bottles of vodka, the three tapes, and the napkin.

When you get right down to it, it was a bit insulting. I mean, I had lots of better things they could have taken. Why the tapes, for God's sake, but not the tape recorder that was lying next to them? Why the napkin, but not the new metal tennis racket or the portable TV?

The worst thing about it was that I had to phone Carlotta, report the loss and ask her if she'd be willing to do the interview, but without the sightseeing tour? She agreed, but if there is anything more tedious than trying to remember three hours of questions and then listening to the answers, I don't want to know about it.

I never again used a tape recorder to do an interview. When God works in concert with Moe, Shemp, and Curly, to drive home a lesson, a person would have to be crazy to ignore it.

The best thing to result from the piece was that Carlotta was then interviewed by Art Linkletter. That led to a book deal, which resulted in a best seller, *W.C. Fields & Me*. That, in turn, led to a movie of the same title starring Rod Steiger as Fields and Valerie Perrine as Carlotta.

Carlotta no longer had to work the night shift at Technicolor.

For a while, after I moved across town, I rarely saw Carlotta. But one day, I received a call from her niece. It seems Carlotta was living in a senior facility in Hollywood, and the niece was sure she'd love to see me. But she warned me that Carlotta might not recognize me.

I wasn't sure I could bear to see her as less than herself. But I manned up and drove over to the facility on Fountain, just off the 101 freeway. I got directions at the reception desk. When I got to her door, I knocked lightly.

When she called out, I entered. Amazingly, she looked unchanged, although it had probably been five years since I'd last seen her. In fact, although she was now in her mid-80s, she looked just as she had when I'd met her twenty years earlier. And when she smiled and said, "Burt, how wonderful to see you!" I couldn't help but wonder what her niece had been talking about. Carlotta was as good as ever.

I sat down and settled in for a visit. When she asked what I was up to, I gave her a brief answer. When I then asked her how she liked living in the facility, she asked me what I was up to. Every minute or so, she would repeat the question, even though I tried to vary my answers.

It finally sank in. Alzheimer's had claimed another victim. She could recognize my face, but that was all.

I stayed for a little while, trying not to cry.

Then I said good-bye.

THE "JUST-THE-FACTS" GUY

Next to being asked how I came by my dashing good looks, the question most often posed to me is how I managed to break into show business.

To the first query, the answer is self-evident: great genes, an exemplary life style, and God's beneficence. In short, you can envy me to your heart's content, but emulation is out of the question.

The second query, as a rule, is proffered by young people anxious to be handed the magic key to the kingdom. Unfortunately, once again they are out of luck. What worked for me is not a blueprint that would work for anyone else.

Lest you think I am behaving like the proverbial dog in the manger, read on.

To set the scene, as it were, by the time opportunity knocked or, in my case, phoned, I was in my late 20s, the century was in its late 60s. I had been working for about eight or nine years as *Los Angeles* magazine's initial movie reviewer, and had also been writing a weekly humor column for the *L.A. Times* for a year or so.

Thanks to a friend's intervention, I had an agent. But, like most of the breed, his primary role in life was to skim ten percent of the money if I or any of his other clients managed to get a job on their own. Towards that end, I was constantly writing sketches for variety shows and spec scripts for my favorite sitcoms, and mailing them to unsuspecting, unresponsive, producers.

The sad fact is that I never heard back from anyone, and had finally concluded that my future with TV would be strictly as a disgruntled viewer.

Then, one morning, I received a call. Because it woke me up from a sound sleep, when the voice introduced itself as Jack Webb, I hung up. My assumption was that the caller was my old UCLA crony, Harry

Shearer, who should have known better than to phone me before nine. I quickly fell back asleep, only to have the phone ring again.

Once more, the voice said: "Hello, this is Jack Webb. I guess we got disconnected."

That woke me up in a hurry. After all, I reasoned, if it had been Harry, the second time around, besides bellyaching about the price of making phone calls, he'd have been "doing" his old standby, *Radioland*'s Paul ("G'Day") Harvey.

I rubbed the sand out of my eyes while Webb explained he was a fan of my humor column and wanted to know if I'd be interested in writing a *Dragnet* episode.

As diplomatically as I could, I explained that whereas I'd been a regular viewer of the earlier *Dragnet*, I hadn't watched its reincarnation. Webb assured me that wasn't a problem. He suggested I drive over to his bungalow on the Universal lot, pick up a few sample scripts, and discuss the particular episode he had in mind.

Meeting Jack was a strange experience. He looked and sounded just the way I'd remembered Sgt. Joe Friday from a decade earlier. What was eerie about it was that over the years, his voice and that delivery had become grist for every impressionist in America. As a result, Jack Webb wound up sounding just like every other guy, including Harry Shearer, "doing" Jack Webb.

So there he was in the flesh, with the same voice, the same crewcut, the same Dumboesque ears.

The episode he had in mind was one in which Friday and his partner, Gannon (a pre- *M*A*S*H* Harry Morgan), would go on a TV panel show and debate the hell out of a couple of cop-hating smarty pants.

No problem. I wrote the script in a few days and, happily, Jack loved it.

Before I knew it, I was up to my eyeballs in *Dragnet*. The system Jack employed was to have cops write up a page or so about a case they had worked. They'd submit the pages to LAPD Lt. Dan Cook, who handled PR for the department. He, in turn, would sift through all the submissions and pass along the 40 or 50 likeliest to Webb. He, in turn, would select his favorites and pass the pages along to his writers.

We were free to contact the cops on the case to find out if there was anything interesting that hadn't made it to the page. After that, our first chore was to disguise the facts sufficiently to ward off possible invasion of privacy lawsuits being filed by the victims or the perps.

For me, the hardest part of writing the show was page length. After that first episode, all the others typically dealt with crimes. But as the show was written in the form of a police report ("9:03: Arrived at Parker Center. Got the call at 9:14: See the man.") nothing could be shown that Friday and Gannon didn't witness with their own eyes. In short, it was a crime show in which you never got to see the planning or commission of a crime.

As a result, when I'd deliver a script, Jack took to holding it at arm's length and declaring that it felt a little light. Well, of course it did. Instead of running 30 pages, my first drafts would run somewhere between 22 and 25. I would explain that there was simply no more material, and suggest that possibly he and Harry could speak more slowly. He'd give me the fish eye and then we'd sit down and add a lot of boring stuff and somehow manage to get the darn thing up to a proper length.

But inasmuch as he never wanted me to flesh out the characters with humor, I once found myself asking Jack why he had approached me, a humorist, in the first place.

"Writing is writing," he explained. "I figured if you could write one thing well, you just might be able to write something else equally well. Besides, it was low risk. If your first script had stunk, I would have cut you off at first draft and we wouldn't have been out very much money. Besides, I had very good luck in the past with newspaper guys. Dick Breen, who wrote almost all the scripts when *Dragnet* was on radio came out of the newspaper racket."

Speaking of the transition from radio to TV, Jack confided that he never really liked acting all that much. When the show transitioned to the tube, Jack had wanted to cast Lloyd Nolan as Sgt. Friday and concentrate on producing and directing. But the sponsor insisted that Jack continue to star.

After I'd written four or five episodes, I paid my agent a visit, pleading with him to get me a shot at a sitcom. I pointed out that I was still writing my humor column for the *L.A. Times* and had now mastered the TV format. Surely there had to be a sit com that would give me an assignment.

I recall he said that the column didn't count, but that with *Dragnet* on my resume, he might be able to get me a *Felony Squad*.

I pointed out that *Felony Squad* wasn't even as good as *Dragnet*, and that at least "Jack lets me come in to the office late on Friday afternoon and drink with him and the cops."

That was true. Jack loved cops, and even though he knew more about police procedure than any of them, he would have a couple around to act as technical advisors, but mainly to drink with them and to hear their cop stories.

Drinking with Jack was definitely a perk of the job and, best of all, was something for which I didn't have to tithe my agent. Although, to tell the truth, there were a few Saturday mornings when I would gladly have given the goniff ten percent of my hangover.

As a rule, late Friday afternoon, the day's shooting over, Jack would open the bar in his office, and whichever cops were working that week as tech advisors would start regaling us with their anecdotes. After a couple of hours, those of us who were still around and awake would adjourn for dinner at either Monty's in Encino, a few blocks from Jack's home, or the China Trader, a restaurant in Toluca Lake that Jack owned. It was where Bobby Troup, the husband of the former Mrs. Jack Webb, Julie London, played piano. Later, Jack would hire both Bobby and Julie to appear on his TV show, *Emergency*.

It struck me as odd at first, but Jack had a soft spot for the people who were raising his two beloved daughters, especially because one of them played great jazz piano. Jack loved jazz.

Life could have gone on that way, if not indefinitely, at least for another year or two. After which, Jack, who liked to work with the same people probably would have had me writing *Adam 12*, but Jack and I reached a bizarre impasse.

By this time, I had written seven or eight *Dragnet* episodes in slightly over a year. In fact, I had just finished my first episode for the new season and had started disguising another storyline in order to avoid one of those pesky invasion of privacy lawsuits when I received an ominous phone call from Jack. This time, I was certain it wasn't Harry Shearer on the line, although I wished it were. Jack said he wanted me to come in and discuss some thoughts he'd had about the latest script.

It wasn't like Jack to interrupt the flow of his assembly line. As I drove over to Universal I couldn't help mulling over what the problem might be. As it turned out, I could have mulled until the cows came home and I would never have guessed.

In the script, the perp had a weakness for bowling. For him, it was a hobby that approached an addiction. In the script, he committed a few crimes involving thefts and cons at bowling alleys. He was even arrested while trying to pick up a 7-10 split, and along the way there was a lot of Friday-Gannon banter revolving around bowling.

Suddenly, I find myself seated across from Webb and he's telling me he wants to change the man's passion from bowling to -- hold on to your hat! --butterflies!

Whereas in the past, I hadn't been able to believe Jack's ears, this time I couldn't believe my own.

Surely, I recall telling myself, the man was making a misguided foray into the land of whimsy. I simply couldn't accept Jack Webb, alias Joe Friday, seriously suggesting we feature butterflies in one of his shows. And yet here he was, patiently explaining that in his grandmother's L.A. boardinghouse, where he'd been raised, one of the boarders had had an extensive butterfly collection and had taught young Jack all about them, including the chemical compounds employed in their preservation.

"Plus," he concluded his sales spiel, putting as much enthusiasm into his usual monotone as he could muster, "in color, we'll get some really beautiful shots."

I granted the aesthetic appeal of butterflies over bowling balls, but wondered why, after approving the earlier drafts of the script, he was suddenly requesting these major revisions. After a good deal of harrumphing around, Jack confessed that he didn't want to go off the Universal lot for a half day's shooting at a North Hollywood bowling alley.

Once I understood the real problem, I was ready with a solution. Through the use of sound effects and a counter full of bowling shoes and score sheets, I pointed out, we could easily indicate the venue in the earlier scenes. And instead of making the arrest just as the perp was picking up a spare, Friday and Gannon could nab him at the coke machine.

This was followed by several seconds of silence, during which I assumed Jack was picturing exactly how he'd shoot the scenes. And perhaps he was, for that's exactly how he wound up shooting the episode. No need to leave the sanctuary of the lot and still able to shoot the whole shebang in a single day. I swear, the man could have taught Henry Ford a thing or two about mass production.

But when he furrowed his brow and got that faraway look in his eyes, it seems he was also envisioning a future that, as Sam Goldwyn might have put it, included Prelutsky out.

It seems that in Jack's world, I had committed the unpardonable sin. The problem wasn't that I had come up with the solution. It was that just prior to solving the dilemma, I had told him that I'd done all the writing on the episode that I was contracted to do -- work that he'd already accepted and approved of -- and that if he insisted on my turning our villain into a butterfly collector, it would entail a page-one rewrite. In short, I would expect to be paid to write that new script.

And so I concluded my apprenticeship. It also served to set the tone for a TV writing career in which I have gotten the Writers Guild to demand penalty payments from Disney, Universal, and Viacom, when those companies tried to get away with financial shenanigans, even though I was told more than once that I'd never again work in this town.

Fortunately, a few months later, I received a phone call one morning. This time it was Leonard Stern, the west coast head of Talent Associates, a production company in which he was partners with David Susskind and Danny Melnick.

Leonard explained that he and his brother-in-law, Budd Schulberg, rarely agreed about anything, but they had recently discovered they both based their movie attendance on my reviews.

He invited me to lunch and then, just before signing off, asked me if I'd be interested in writing an episode of his Dan Dailey-Julie Sommars sitcom, *The Governor and J.J.*

As diplomatically as I could, I explained that I'd never watched the show.

But that's another story.

THE UNLIKELY EXORCIST

I have no idea when William Peter Blatty and I became friends, and whether someone introduced us or if we simply ran into each other and hit it off. What I do know is that it was nearly 50 years ago and, although we are now separated by a continent, we are still friends.

Back when we first became pals, Bill was a successful humorist best known for a couple of books (*Which Way to Mecca, Jack and John Goldfarb, Please Come Home*) and some movies (*A Shot in the Dark* and *Promise Her Anything*), but it was his impersonation of a black sheep from the royal family of Saudi Arabia, Prince Xeer, that had captured my attention.

Back in the 1950's, while working in the publicity department at USC, Bill got the notion of passing himself off as this mysterious figure, whom he once described to me as being illiterate in both Arabic and English. He got a friend to act as his bodyguard/translator in this absurd enterprise.

Bill, whose parents were Lebanese, was Hollywood handsome with black hair and blue eyes. But nobody saw his eyes because, as the Prince, he always wore sunglasses. Although his translator never really spelled out why the Prince had been exiled to America, he broadly hinted that Bill had killed someone in Saudi Arabia and his parents thought it would be a good idea if he let things cool down before returning.

The people to whom these hints were dropped tended to be the maître 'ds at the various nightclubs that were flourishing in L.A. at the time -- places like Ciro's, the Trocadero, and the Mocambo. Bill's stooge would make a point of asking when they were born and would then jot down the dates in a little notebook. As a result, every guy who wore a tux to work on the Sunset Strip imagined he was going to receive a Rolls Royce on his birthday. In appreciation, Bill and his friend ate and drank to their heart's content and never received a bill.

God only knows how long the farce might have gone on, but Bill was a writer and he couldn't resist telling all in an article he published in the *Saturday Evening Post*.

One of the anecdotes he shared in the piece was that he had been invited to dine at the home of Dick Powell and June Allyson, and that when Prince Xeer began to eat the salad with his hands, his host and hostess, wishing to put him at ease, set aside their forks and they, too, ate the salad with their hands.

When I asked Bill if there had been any repercussions to the stunt, he said that he received a phone call at his USC office soon after the article ran. It was Dick Powell inviting him to dinner. The catch was he had to show up as the Prince, not as Bill Blatty.

Once he began writing *The Exorcist*, all the laughter seemed to go out of him. We would make plans to go out to dinner and I'd show up at the A-frame he was renting in the hills and find him gloomy and frustrated. He would groan and gripe that he should never have accepted an advance from the publisher. Once he even showed me the proposed book cover. It didn't look like the cover of any best seller I had ever seen.

Each time he would say "Why did I ever start this? I'm a comedy writer. What the hell am I doing writing a book about an exorcism?" And each time, I would say, "Why bother? It's ruining your life. Give them back their advance and toss the pages in your fireplace."

For a minute, he would look tempted. Then the moment would pass and we'd go out to dinner.

At the time, Bill and I were with the same talent agency. Each time I would show up at their office in Westwood, they would ask me to remind Bill that his contract was about to end and that he should come in and renew.

I would then remind Bill and he would say that he would, but that he was busy with the book and rarely got to Westwood.

To this day, I don't know if it was ever his intention to renew, but it certainly saved him a few bucks. Instead of having to fork over 10% when he signed with Warner's to adapt and produce *The Exorcist*, he had his lawyer represent him.

With the publication of the novel, which would remain on the best seller list for over a year, Bill's life changed radically. He moved away from California, bought homes in various places, got married and had two sons.

But before he took off, I received a call from the publisher's publicist, asking if I'd care to interview Bill for my column in the *L.A. Times*. I assured him I would. I had already supplied them with a blurb for the book: "Be sure to read *The Exorcist* with every light on in your house and every light on in your brain."

It wasn't just hyperbole, either. It was the most frightening book I had ever read, not to mention the most psychologically gripping. Although I was happy for Bill that the movie was such a success, garnering him an Oscar for his script, I didn't find the movie scary. In fact, I actually laughed out loud a couple of times, such as when the victim's head spun like a top and when what looked suspiciously like pea soup spewed out of her mouth.

What I had experienced when reading Bill's words on the page just seemed hokey on screen.

When I phoned Bill to set up the interview, he'd have none of it. "I have a better idea," he said. Of course he did. After all, this was the same man -- a little older, a lot richer and more famous -- but still the same mind that had come up with Prince Xeer.

His plan was for me to come up to his place and do the interview the day before we met. Then when we got together for the pretend interview, in the presence of the publicist, Blatty the Lebanese and Prelutsky the Jew would get into a fierce argument, and that I would then stomp out of the restaurant while the publicist swallowed his own tongue.

It struck me as a little bit cruel, but, on the other hand, the guy got paid very well for a job that, when you got right down to it, consisted of having lunch with writers and reporters.

So it was, that the following day, I showed up at the Tail O' the Cock restaurant in the San Fernando Valley, pen and steno book in hand. The publicist introduced me to Bill, I sat down, opened the notebook, poised to ask my first question when, right on cue, Bill said something unkind about Israel. I returned the fire. He escalated and I followed suit. All the while, the publicist's eyes widened, his mouth opened, but no words emerged. Just a few gasping noises.

Finally, I stood up from the booth and started walking away. I had taken only a few steps when I heard what sounded like…. giggling. I turned around and, sure enough, the man who had fooled half of Hollywood into believing he was an Arab on the lam, was giggling like a school girl!

The charade over, I returned to the booth. Bill was wiping his eyes, but I noticed that the publicist continued to look like a stone carving. Apparently, he hadn't yet caught on. I explained that I had already done the interview and that it would appear about a week later in the *L.A. Times*.

He didn't laugh, but at least he resumed breathing after a fashion. His eyes, though, continued to appear glazed with shock.

In the years since, Bill has written several more books and even directed some movies, including sequels to *The Exorcist*. Unfortunately, he now lives in Bethesda, Maryland. It's not too far away from where a priest first told Bill the story of a real life exorcism that planted the fatal seed.

I've often wondered what would have happened if I'd persuaded Bill to toss the unfinished manuscript in the fire. Surely, he, his publisher and Warner Brothers would be out several million dollars, but Blatty and I probably wouldn't have to resort to email to stay in touch. And there's a certain book publicist who wouldn't have had a good ten or twenty years knocked off his life span.

DRESS ENGLISH, THINK YIDDISH

When I was a young advertising copywriter, my first boss, the creative director at the agency gave me those four words of advice. Although the Yiddish part came naturally, I never did dress English. Perhaps that's why my advertising career was so short-lived.

Somewhere along the line, though, it had become the motto of writer-producer Leonard Stern.

Although our getting together for lunch had been the result of Leonard's discovering that both he and his brother-in-law Budd Schulberg used my reviews as their movie guide, the conversation had mainly been about him. It was always his favorite topic. In time, I came to believe that it wasn't just run-of-the-mill egotism. I think he truly marveled at the cosmopolitan creature he had created.

In the late 40s, as I discovered from photos, Leonard had been a flabby-faced New Yorker in a cheap suit who looked like he sold stolen goods from the trunk of an old Buick. By the time I knew him, he had a closet that must have rivaled Joan Crawford's, spoke with a mid-Atlantic accent, grown a fashionable beard, lost at least 30 pounds and looked like he had stepped out of an *Esquire* ad.

As part of the image, he drove a Mercedes. Unfortunately, it was the smallest model they produced, so when he was at the wheel, he cut quite a dashing figure, but when he got out of it by unwinding all 6'2" of himself, he looked like the last clown emerging from the circus car.

Stern had broken into the business writing gags for radio comedians, which led to assignments on Ma & Pa Kettle and Abbott & Costello movies. He finally came into his own writing for TV, where his writing credits included Steve Allen's variety show, *Sgt. Bilko* and *The Honeymooners*. Soon he was producing and directing as well, and as a partner in Talent Associates, achieved his greatest success producing *Get Smart*.

By the time we had lunch, he had only one show on the air, *The Governor & J.J.*, starring Dan Dailey and Julie Sommars as the title characters. He asked me if I'd care to try writing an episode. I jumped at the chance to finally write a sitcom, even though I had to confess I wasn't familiar with the series. Fortunately, the script came off well and I hit it off with the episode's guest star, Jack Cassidy.

It led to a night of drinking with Cassidy and his pal Jack Weston. The next day I recalled we laughed a lot, but that's all I recall.

It also led to Stern offering me a job. I think he said I would help him develop shows, but in reality I suspect he saw me in the role of Boswell to his Samuel Johnson, following him around with a notebook recording his bon mots for posterity. Although he was amiable, he was hardly another Oscar Wilde, or Samuel Johnson for that matter, so it would have been a very short book. It wasn't that Leonard wasn't bright, but he thought it was hilarious if someone said it was a nice day and Leonard, playing the role of God, would say: "You're welcome." Sometimes, though, you couldn't be sure he knew he was just playing the role.

Although I'm pretty certain it wasn't the fault of my episode, *The Governor & J.J.* was cancelled before I had the chance to write a second one. Fortunately, Leonard, who was a born salesman, soon sold NBC on a new series.

By that time, I was ensconced in my own office on the ground floor of a two-story bungalow on the CBS lot, in Studio City. Upstairs, the Mary Tyler Moore company had its offices. It never seemed right that even with all their shows, we had the same amount of space they did. I kept expecting they would expand into our space and we would wind up in a broom closet.

I made it a practice to always leave my office door open. It wasn't that I was claustrophobic, but the view outside my window was a parking lot.

The new series was to be called *McMillan & Wife*. As you can see, the ampersand played a very big role in Stern's career. Other instances were such short-lived TV series as *He & She, Faraday & Company, Holmes & Yo-Yo,* and *Rosetti & Ryan.*

What I knew about the new series was that it would star Rock Hudson and that they hadn't yet cast Mrs. McMillan. But it wasn't for want of trying. Each day, I would see young actresses pass by my open door on their way to Stern's office at the end of the corridor. NBC or Universal Studios was even flying them in from New York. On consecutive days, I saw Jill Clayburgh and Sigourney Weaver make their way past my door.

In the end, the search ended when someone realized that Hudson was already costing them $150,000-an-episode and maybe it would be a good idea if they used one of Universal's reasonably-priced contract players. And that, boys and girls, is how Susan St. James got the role.

One morning, on his way down the corridor, Leonard Stern stuck his head in and said that if I got any ideas for *McMillan*, I should write them down and perhaps I would get a shot at writing the script.

Well, I suppose in retrospect, I should have asked more questions. But what I knew was that Mr. McMillan, "Mac," was the commissioner of police in San Francisco and his wife, Sally, was a housewife who would meddle in his crime-solving affairs. It never made any sense to me that the lead would be a police commissioner since solving crimes is not their function. As for Sally, her main purpose was to share banter with Mac.

But her secondary function was to get herself into jeopardy so that her husband could rescue her. In one episode, she was being held hostage in a warehouse on the docks. Mac gets wind of her location. When he shows up, he finds that the villain has shot and killed a cop. Then, without stooping to pick up the officer's revolver, he rushes in to confront the villain. In spite of the bad guy having a loaded gun, Mac wins the day, knocking him out and rescuing Sally.

The morning after seeing the show, I asked Stern why, with the cop's gun in plain sight, they'd had Mac ignore it and plunge ahead to confront an armed criminal? He explained that Rock Hudson was so big, he couldn't also have a gun or he wouldn't appear heroic.

In any case, at the time Leonard had suggested I try my hand at coming up with an idea, the show hadn't been on the air and I hadn't read the pilot script because it hadn't yet been written. The one thing I had no doubts about, though, was that the show was a sitcom. After all, that's what Leonard did. I therefore assumed that the couple would only get involved in minor crimes that would allow them a lot of opportunities within the 24-minute time frame for lively banter. It just made sense that radio's *Mr. & Mrs. North* was Leonard's model. Or perhaps, as it turned out, because they drank quite a bit, maybe it was Nick and Nora Charles that he had in mind.

In any case, by lunchtime, I had come up with a one-page idea. Basically, my episode would deal with a neighbor's dog being kidnapped or, more properly, dognapped. Plenty of room for lively banter.

Leonard read the page, looked up, smiled, and said, "I like it." Then, spreading his hands wide, he said, "Now you just need to make it bigger."

"No," I recall saying, "I think that's enough plot for a sitcom."

"But, *McMillan* isn't a sitcom. It's going to be 90 minutes long. NBC is going to put it in its Wednesday night Mystery Wheel, alternating it with a few other mystery shows."

"Really?" I said. "I had no idea. Well, in that case, I better start over. You can't very well devote ninety minutes to a stolen dog."

"No, I like that part. You just need to expand on it."

I trudged back to my office, the corridor feeling a lot like the last mile in the big house that mugs like Jimmy Cagney, George Raft, and Eddie G. Robinson used to walk on their way to the hot seat.

But necessity, as they say, is the mother-in-law of invention. What I finally cobbled together was a story in which a neighbor of Sally's mother reports that her beloved dog has been kidnapped, but so has her husband…but it's only the dog's ransom she wishes to pay.

Somehow, by sticking in a couple of murders, the script got written.

The next time that Stern stuck his head in my office, I should have ducked under my desk. But hindsight is always 20-20.

This time, it was a Monday morning. Over the weekend, Leonard had been at a party and run into George Burns. Burns let him know that he was a big fan of *McMillan* and would love to be in an episode. What's more, Leonard reported, Burns had said if he agreed to do it, he could get Jack Benny to join him because he could get Jack to do anything.

So Leonard set me to work. As I recall, he also suggested the story be set at a race track.

What I came up with was a murder that took place at a track and involved jockeys, stewards, bookies and doped horses. I had Burns and Benny as a pair of estranged brothers. Burns was the natty one who ran the racetrack, Benny was the cheap one who owned a horse. The McMillan connection was that as a little girl, Sally had grown up on an adjoining ranch and had been very fond of the Benny character and realized that the cheapness, along with his gruffness, was just an image he fostered.

Well, as someone once said, life is what happens while you're making other plans. What happened in this case is that George Burns won an Oscar for his role in *Oh, God!* Suddenly, he was a hot item and in no mood to appear in a TV episode.

So, no George Burns, no Jack Benny. But TV is like a train and it has a schedule to keep. In fact, I've always said, the miracle isn't that TV fare is sometimes very good, but that, in spite of everything that can go wrong, if a show is scheduled to go on at 9 p.m. on Wednesday night, when you turn on your set, there it is.

Going on in place of George Burns was an Australian actor named Murray Matheson, while William Demarest would be stepping in for Jack Benny.

It was awful. For one thing, there wasn't time for me to rewrite the dialogue or alter the characters. I was stuck with these two, one of them sounding like a posh Englishman, the other sounding like he had grown up on the lower eastside of New York. Making it even worse is that by this time, Demarest, who had been wonderful 30 years earlier in such Preston Sturges comedy classics as *Hail the Conquering*

Hero and *The Miracle of Morgan's Creek*, was now quite old and couldn't remember his lines.

The best I can say for the episode is that when millions of people turned on their sets to watch it, there it was right on schedule. The worst I can say for it is that when millions of people turned on their sets to watch it, there it was.

At the same time that I was working for Stern, I was writing my column for the *L.A. Times*. One week, the person I was set to interview had to bow out at the last second. In a panic, and without time to arrange another interview, I made up a person and interviewed "him."

The character I invented was triggered by another show on the mystery wheel, *McCloud* which starred Dennis Weaver as a western marshal who is given a temporary assignment in New York City, the old fish out of water device.

My creation was a New York police detective who is fed up with life in the big city and has been paying off on acreage in Arizona to which he plans to retire and raise oranges. However, when he gets there, he discovers he's been had, and that the only things you could raise on the land are cactus and iguanas.

In desperation, he accepts a job as the local sheriff.

The deception worked better than I imagined because Stern had cut the article out of the paper and took it along to NBC where he sold them on the idea of doing it as a TV movie, with a series to follow.

Brock never made it to a series, perhaps because they cast Richard Widmark in the title role. Widmark was a good enough dramatic actor, but he had the comic touch of Rasputin on a bad hair day.

Leonard Stern had helped me pay my rent for three years, but money finally wasn't enough. Even I was surprised when he took me along to a network meeting where he was going to discuss a new series he was going to do with John Astin, based on the Cary Grant-Tony Curtis movie *Operation Petticoat*.

As I recall, Leonard was going to make me story editor or some such thing. But at some point, not having planned it, I suddenly stood up, said, "Excuse me," and announced I wasn't going to be involved in the enterprise. When I turned to leave the room, someone asked me why not, and again without having planned to say it, I replied: "Because I want to be the one who decides what's funny, not Leonard."

I didn't intend to have it come out sounding insulting, and I guess Leonard understood that because we remained on friendly terms for years afterward.

I guess we both understood that I would never be his Boswell.

BROWN-EYED SUSAN

One can never predict how seemingly unrelated events will influence your life. For instance, when I got an assignment from *TV Guide* to profile Robert Stack, the major impression it had on me was one of fear. The reason was that I was told he was filming the pilot for a new TV series in Santa Monica Bay, and that I would have to be transported from a little boat to the somewhat larger boat he'd be on.

It was just too obvious to me that I could easily mess up while trying to stand up in one boat bobbing on the waves to climb aboard a second boat bobbing in the waves, and wind up either drowning in the ocean or being fished out and trying to conduct an interview while sopping wet and freezing.

Fortunately, I managed to clamber aboard, did the interview and managed to get home without even getting my feet wet.

Writing for *TV Guide* was a snap. It consisted of doing a sit-down with the subject, then filling in some gaps with a few of their friends or associates, and a thousand words later, you were done.

Sometimes, of course, unforeseen problems would crop up. For instance, once I was supposed to profile John Amos, a black actor on *Good Times*. When I showed up, he refused to talk to me, claiming he would only agree to be interviewed by a black writer.

Another time, my assignment was Rowan and Martin. That time, Dick Martin refused to talk to me, except to say he would only agree to be profiled for *TV Guide* when the magazine agreed to list the show as *Rowan & Martin's Laugh-In* in the log. I pointed out that, one, I had nothing to do with the listing, and, two, that I was sure it was just a matter of space and no personal animus that had them limit the listing to *Laugh In*.

"I don't care," he said as he turned around and walked away. Hard to argue with "I don't care."

131

Another time, my subject was Marlo Thomas. ABC had approached her to produce and star in a Christmas special. She had asked her friends for suggestions, and several of them had told her that *It's a Wonderful Life* was their favorite Christmas story.

Apparently, she had never even heard of the classic. But she got hold of a copy and, after seeing it, decided that all it needed was a little tweaking to make her version better than the original.

The little tweaking the feminist nitwit had in mind was to reverse the sexes. In her version, she would have the Jimmy Stewart role, George Bailey, or in this case Mary Bailey Hatch, be the one who loses her faith and then regains it one Christmas Eve. In the role of the spouse played by Donna Reed, Marlo had cast Wayne Rogers. As the Angel, formerly Clarence Oddbody, she had inserted Cloris Leachman, renamed Clara Oddbody.

Only Orson Welles got to play a role originally cast with a male, Lionel Barrymore, filling in as Henry Potter. I can only imagine she hadn't gotten an actress to portray Henrietta Potter because it would have anguished her feminist sensibilities to cast a woman as a greedy, cold-hearted wretch.

When I told Marlo that *It's a Wonderful Life* was one of my own all-time favorite movies and I could not see how TV could possibly improve on the Frank Capra classic, she actually said, "Ours is way better."

I finally saw it, and it wasn't. In fact, it was even worse than I imagined because, in keeping with Marlo's sexist agenda, she, too, took over the small town savings and loan created by her father, even though her movie, too, was set in the 1930s, when such things simply didn't happen.

What's more, she didn't even have a character in the movie comment on how unusual it was that this little woman was assuming the burden. To even bring it up, I suppose, would have violated Marlo's core beliefs.

In any case, what disturbed Marlo was that in the course of filling out the piece, I quoted a couple of unnamed associates who shared with me that, having worked with her, they thought she was an okay actress, but a menace to mankind or, rather, womankind, as a boss. One of them even squealed and told me that Marlo had told her underlings that yellow was her color, and that any woman in her office who dared wear yellow would be fired on the spot!

A few days after meeting with Marlo, I received a phone call from my editor back in Radnor, PA. He told me he was a friend of Phil Donahue, who was engaged to Marlo at the time. The two guys were in the habit of having lunch once a week in Philadelphia, where Donahue filmed his afternoon TV talk show. This time, when they met, even before shaking hands, Donahue demanded to know if Marlo was getting the cover.

For what it's worth, every one of my profiles got the *TV Guide* cover up to then. But, *TV Guide* hated being pressured. Marlo didn't get the cover.

Prior to filing the story, I had called Marlo and asked if she wanted to explain or deny her insisting that none of her secretaries or assistants could wear yellow to the office. Instead of commenting or denying, though, she demanded to know who had told me. I explained that I had promised not to divulge their identities, as they feared reprisals.

I again asked her if she was denying the allegation, but she ignored the question, instead demanding that I cough up their names, each time raising the decibel level. Finally, I broke into her tirade long enough to point out that I didn't work for her and, therefore, I could wear yellow if I felt like it and, what's more, I could hang up on her. Which I did.

The follow-up with Robert Stack was not dissimilar except that it took place in person.

His complaint was that in the article, I had written two things that annoyed him. I couldn't figure out why he was annoyed that, although, he was proud to have received a supporting actor Oscar nomination for *Written on the Wind*, he was so ashamed of winning an Emmy for *The Untouchables*, that he hid it in a closet. The only reason I knew about this was because he had told me. I guess he assumed it was to be our little secret. It seems he considered himself a movie star, and the Emmy for a TV role reminded him that he no longer was.

The other thing he objected to was my quoting an unnamed acquaintance who said that Stack and his wife Rosemarie Bowes were such social butterflies that they would show up for the opening of an envelope.

When he spotted me at a party he made a beeline in my direction, all but breathing fire through his nostrils. He demanded to know who had said it. I told Stack I had promised not to give up his name and I wasn't about to go back on my word. I told him I was sure that my readers understood it was only an expression and that he and this missus didn't really dress up and go out for envelope openings.

The two good things I recall about that night were, one, that Stack didn't punch me and two, that one of the other guests was Susan Strasberg, who decided I was both cute and funny.

I thought she was cute. And as neither of us was married at the time, we began dating. Frankly, I knew before meeting her that she was pretty and, I assumed, intelligent. But I was surprised that she was funny. She always seemed so serious in movies. Besides, she had introduced Anne Frank to Broadway audiences. You can't get more serious than that. On top of which, her father was the pre-eminent acting coach in America, Lee Strasberg. In certain circles, they constituted a form of theatrical royalty. But I wasn't intimidated.

Susan was something of a godsend because I was just coming out of an awful marriage and a gut-wrenching divorce/custody fight.

Early on, she confided that she and her brother rather resented the love and attention that their father lavished on the two boys he had sired by his second wife. Strasberg, like many other men in show business, was so busy pursuing his career and making his name that the first kids got short shrift. But with the next wife or even the wife after that, these guys are older, settled, and they just naturally adopt a role that is closer to that of grandfather than father.

The other thing that annoyed Susan was that Tony Musante, who had starred as her husband on *Toma*, had decided that he was too great an actor to waste his time and talent on a TV series, even a successful one. The reason for Susan's justifiable anger was that her contract only brought her $1,500-a-week that first season. If Musante hadn't decided he was the second coming of Marlon Brando, in a second season, her salary would have jumped to $10,000-a-week.

Instead, Robert Blake got the *Toma* timeslot and got wealthy doing *Baretta*. Unfortunately, Susan didn't get to play Mrs. Baretta. Baretta didn't have a wife, he had a parrot.

Susan and I got along fine, except that she was often taking off for New York. But anyone will tell you that dating an actress, especially one who has been denied a few hundred thousand dollars a year because of an actor's ego, can be a handful. But, then, so can I.

On one memorable occasion, she took me to a party held at the home of Diane Ladd, mother of Laura Dern, ex-wife of Bruce Dern. On the drive over, Susan alerted me that Ms. Ladd was dying to produce and star in a movie about Martha Mitchell, the eccentric, hard-drinking wife of Richard Nixon's attorney general, John Mitchell.

The guest of honor was a very wealthy older gay southern gentleman, who every six months or so left his very staid community to give vent to his secret yearnings, so to speak, in New York or L.A. Diane Ladd was hoping to entice him to invest a few million dollars in her pet project.

While Susan spent most of the evening chatting with Diane, I spent most of my time talking to a writer who had just won an Oscar for his screenplay. I assume Diane Ladd had him in mind to write the Martha Mitchell script.

On the way home, Susan asked me if I'd had a good time. I said it had been okay. I told her I thought the Oscar winner was an interesting guy. I wondered if he was gay. She gazed at me as if I had just landed here -- kerplunk! -- from a very distant planet. I asked her why she was giving me that funny look.

"You mean you didn't realize you were the only straight man at the party?"

What could I say? Apparently I'd led a very sheltered life.

What finally killed the relationship was that she had begun writing her memoir, *Bittersweet*. I thought it was interesting, although perhaps leaning a little too much on her friendship with one of her father's acting students, Marilyn Monroe. But even those chapters had a few gems. I still remember her writing about the two of them walking unnoticed through the streets of New York one afternoon. At one point, Marilyn decided to show off for Susan by turning herself into "Marilyn." I suspect it involved changing her walk. Whatever it was, within minutes, they were surrounded by a frenzied mob of fans.

My problem with the book is that Susan felt obliged to write about an affair she had had with Richard Burton while appearing with him and Helen Hayes on Broadway in Jean Anouilh's *Time Remembered*. She had already told me about the affair between the 18-year-old ingénue and the 32-year-old actor, and how they would be aware that Ms. Hayes was listening at the door trying to catch them in the act.

My objection to her writing about it was that Burton was still married to his first wife, Sybil, at the time, and I saw no reason why all these years later Susan should hurt her or their two daughters by blabbing about committing adultery with their husband/father.

I have on other occasions marveled at the fact that after a certain age, female celebrities will often write tell-all books, as if the world needed to be reminded that they had once been sexy, desirable women. I just thought that Susan was still a little young to be doing it and, I had believed, a little too nice.

She disagreed.

The one real downside to our time together was that for some reason, she refused to bathe her dog. Years later, I heard from a mutual friend that after Susan had moved back to Manhattan, her dog inexplicably leaped through the window of her fifth story apartment to his death.

I assumed the smell had simply gotten to be too much, and the depressed little dog had committed suicide.

Because I had missed reading about it, I had been unaware that Susan had died of cancer at the age of 60. I first learned of her death while watching the Oscars and seeing her included in the "In Memoriam" section, discovering she had passed just a couple of months before.

It had been 20 years since I'd seen her, but it still felt like a punch to my heart.

SNAPSHOTS IV

Although I was born in Chicago, we moved when I was six. But in spite of growing up in L.A., I didn't see my first celebrities until I was 12-years-old. The sightings came about because my best friend sold the Sunday *L.A. Times* in Beverly Hills. He didn't deliver them, though, he just had the northwest corner of Wilshire and Canon. One summer, he was going off on a week vacation with his family and asked me to fill in for him.

He didn't have a newspaper stand, he just had the corner. So there would be these two large piles of newspaper. I would sit on one and read a book, and when a customer would walk over, I'd hand him a paper from the second pile without standing up, and he would hand me, as I recall, a quarter.

The first time I looked up and recognized someone, it was Orson Bean. Although he wasn't famous at the time, I recognized him from having seen him performing his stand-up comedy routine on TV shows out of New York, like the *Blue Angel*. Part of his routine was to create a Christmas tree out of a newspaper while he was telling jokes.

I had no idea what he was doing in L.A., but I assumed he was staying at the nearby Beverly Wilshire Hotel. I wanted to ask him if he wanted to read the *Times* or was just buying it so he could take it back to his hotel room and practice turning it into a Christmas tree, but I was too shy.

But being shy beat the shit out of being scared out of my wits by my next celebrity customer. I first became aware that someone wanted to buy a newspaper when I noticed a pair of black shoes and black cuffs appearing below my book. I looked up. Above the black slacks was a red jacket. Above the red jacket was what appeared to be a skull gazing down at me. It was Jack Palance, whom I recognized from *Panic in the Streets* and *Sudden Fear*.

Between the red jacket, the black hair, the hollow cheeks and the deep-set eyes, if he were auditioning to play Satan, I'd have hired him on the spot.

I was relieved when he moved on. Apparently, the devil hadn't shown up to collect my measly little soul and cart it off to Hades.

I would encounter both Bean and Palance years later. In the case of Palance, I would be interviewing him for some magazine or other. The interview might have gone better if he hadn't kept looking around for Carol Lynley, with whom he was shooting a TV movie. He didn't seem even slightly fazed by the 23-year discrepancy in their ages. He also didn't seem to mind letting me know that he would have very much preferred having lunch with her. But, then, so would I.

I wouldn't run into Orson Bean for decades. Then it was only our politics that brought us together. There are more Republicans than you would ever imagine lurking in Hollywood, and the reason you wouldn't imagine it is because, with few exceptions, if word got out, they could kiss their careers good-bye.

Hollywood liberals are extremely tolerant of their fellow human beings, so long as those people happen to be blacks, Muslims or gays. Not so much if they're Republicans.

Over the years, I would meet a great many of the actors, actresses, directors, composers, who had provided me with so much entertainment over the years. After a while, I stopped being so shy around them. They were, after all, just people. Talented people, yes, but, otherwise, just people.

On occasion, I would be nervous before going off to interview them. The problem was that I was afraid if I didn't like them in person, it might ruin their work in my eyes. For instance, I never met Humphrey Bogart, but what if I had and decided he was a jerk. How could that help but ruin future viewings of *The Maltese Falcon*, *Casablanca*, and *The African Queen*, for me?

***

That's how I felt when his P.R. man approached me about interviewing Jimmy Stewart. Although I hadn't really liked his later westerns, some of his movies, *You Can't Take It with You*, *Mr. Smith Goes to Washington*, *It's a Wonderful Life*, even *Harvey*, were among my all-time favorites. What if he was the opposite of that decent American we had all come to see as the idealized version of our best selves?

The day before we were set to meet, his P.R. man called to ask if I would mind postponing the get-together. It seemed that one of his beloved step-sons, Marine 1st Lt. Ron McLean, had been killed in Vietnam.

I assumed Stewart would want to postpone it a month, but it was just a matter of days before he welcomed me into his home. I said a few words of condolence for his loss, but Stewart, who had flown a bomber in World War II, said, "Ron was where he wanted to be, doing what he felt needed to be done."

Coming from Stewart, it sounded like he meant it.

It was a pleasant two-story home, unpretentious by Beverly Hills standards, the sort of homey place you would picture Jimmy Stewart living in.

At one point I asked him if he minded being regarded as absent-minded. "It doesn't bother me. I guess it sort of goes with the slow way I have of speaking, but I really don't know why I have that reputation. Although there was this one time. Gloria was in the hospital. She'd just delivered our twins. She was packing up and I went downstairs to drive the car around.

For some reason, I drove to our neighborhood camera shop to pick up some pictures I'd dropped off to be developed. When the proprietor asked how Gloria was doing, I said, 'Whoops!' I drove back to the hospital.

She and the babies were waiting at the curb. But that's the only thing that comes to mind."

***

141

When you first meet some of the legends, it's almost surreal. Take Bob Hope. One of my earliest memories was of hearing his voice on the radio when we were still living in Chicago, a city we left just after I turned six.

If you were born in 1940, Bob Hope had seemingly been a part of your life one way or another forever. Between radio, movies, TV, newsreels, and emceeing the Oscars 19 times, "Old Ski Nose" always seemed to be around. If he wasn't good-naturedly kidding a president, he was amusing thousands of G.I.s by making wisecracks about the brass, while inviting the grunts to ogle Marilyn Maxwell or the most recent Miss America; or losing Dorothy Lamour to Bing Crosby; or singing his signature song, "Thanks for the Memory." I even recalled seeing a version of Bob Hope showing up in a couple of cartoons.

The way he kept popping up in war zones during WWII, Korea, and Vietnam, it was as if he was the USO! That's why meeting him was a lot like being in the presence of an animatronic, like a flesh and blood version of the Abraham Lincoln attraction at Disneyland. Hell, it was almost like interviewing the Grand Canyon or the Washington Monument.

I knew the usual stuff going in. I knew this most American of comics, with his fast-talking delivery and his skirt-chasing image, truer than most of his fans ever imagined, had been born in England. I knew he had been a boxer in his teens, fighting under the name of Packy East.

Because I knew a few of his former writers, Roger Price, Mort Lachman, and Mel Shavelson, I also knew that he paid his staff the most in the business, but in return you had to be on call 24/7 in case he found himself accepting a request to speak at a charity event and needed half an hour of "ad libs." I also knew that he was actually paid to speak at these events and that, on occasion, his fee amounted to more than even his presence brought in for the charity.

Rumor had it that Hope had wisely invested his money in real estate and wound up owning the half of the San Fernando Valley not owned by Fred MacMurray, but the truth is he probably only owned a third of it.

I also knew that he used to stand on a balcony overlooking his living room at Christmas time and toss the writers their bonus checks in envelopes and watch them scramble on the floor to retrieve them.

Royalty will have its little whims.

The truth is, I have little recollection of what Bob Hope said that afternoon, but I don't fault him for it. I had discovered that in some cases, when people have been in the spotlight for decades, their responses are all canned because they have been asked the same or similar questions ten thousand times in the past. Their disinterest can be contagious.

What I recall best from the experience of our time in his Toluca Lake home was that he had a nine-hole golf course in his backyard and a framed, autographed photo of Gen. George Patton on his wall. It showed old "Blood & Guts" standing in full battle regalia on the side of the Rhine, urinating into the river.

Although it wasn't one of my more memorable interviews, I surprised myself when, several years later, I was driving my car and heard a news flash that Bob Hope had just died. Without warning, I felt the tears well up. I actually had to pull over before I crashed.

He was 95, so it wasn't as if it was entirely unexpected. But it felt as if I had just gotten word that an old friend or a member of the family had died. In a way, Bob Hope was a little of both.

Later that day, the world learned it had been a false rumor. Something Hope had eaten had disagreed with him, but it was nothing serious.

His daughter reported that her father had laughed when he heard the report. But inasmuch as word had gotten out only after a couple of lamebrain politicians had reported the non-event on the floor of Congress, Hope probably figured it was par for the course.

He would live a few more years, making it all the way to 100. It seemed appropriate. After all, eras are often broken down by centuries, and the 20th had certainly been Bob Hope's.

***

Another legend was Eddie G. Robinson. I had gotten his phone number from someone and had tried, unsuccessfully, to reach him. Then one day, when I was working at Talent Associates, a secretary came into a meeting to let me know I had a call. Robinson was on the line. Everyone in the room turned to look at me as if I were playing a practical joke. Even I felt as if it was a prank.

But it was Little Caesar himself, inviting me out to his house.

My first impression of the man was that he was tiny. I mean, I was only 5'7 and I could see the top of his head. It made it even more impressive that for 40 years he had commanded the screen, the focus of everyone's attention, no matter who else was in the scene.

To me, one of the things that makes Academy Awards so problematic was that in spite of someone like Lana Turner having been nominated twice for Oscars, Eddie G. Robinson hadn't ever been nominated, not for *Little Caesar*, not for *Dr. Ehrlich's Magic Bullet*, not for *The Sea Wolf*, not for *Woman in the Window*, not for *Our Vines Have Tender Grapes*, not even for *Double Indemnity*.

The most amazing part of being in his home was the artwork on the walls. Although I had heard that he and Billy Wilder had the two greatest collections in Hollywood, it is one thing to read about it and quite another to see paintings you had only seen in books hanging on the walls.

When I asked him how he had come to own such a collection, he said that when he began making money he started buying paintings, not as an investment, but simply because he loved the work so much that he wanted to live surrounded by it.

Billy Wilder had given me much the same answer. But later in life, just out of curiosity, Wilder had decided to have his own collection appraised. When he learned it was worth something like $35 million, he decided to sell, keeping a few precious pieces for himself and donating some of the paintings to an Israeli museum. It was much more than he had ever made making movies, he reported, the surprise still evident in his voice.

At one point, as I was about to leave, Eddie invited me to cross the bridge over his driveway that connected his house to a room in which he kept his most valuable oils.

Although I was only able to spend a minute or so because I was running late for a meeting, stepping into the room was a shock. The four walls were covered by scores of famous paintings. At the far end, perhaps 50 feet away, in the place of honor, was a large painting of what appeared to be a sunflower. Because of its surroundings, I assumed it to be a Van Gogh, although I wasn't aware that he had ever painted anything that huge.

A few years later, I was talking to a local painter. When I mentioned my visit to Robinson's home, she mentioned that she, too, had been there for a visit. She brought up that very painting and asked if I had seen it.

I mentioned I had, but only from a distance.

She said it had been painted by Mrs. Robinson. "You could see by the painting that she was clearly insane."

Since I hadn't met the woman, I couldn't comment. But since the painter who had obviously been her inspiration had sliced off his own ear, it didn't seem to be an unreasonable conclusion.

**

I knew, because W.C. Fields's long-time lady friend Carlotta Monti had told me so, that Fields couldn't stand Mae West. But I was still curious about meeting her.

So I arranged an interview at the Ravenswood, a high-rise apartment house that she owned and where she lived.

When I took the self-service elevator up to her floor, I took a few last drags on my cigarette before rubbing it out in the sand-filled canister in the corridor. I had been warned that Ms. West did not allow smoking in her presence.

What I hadn't been warned of before stepping into her apartment was the risk of snow-blindness. It was all white. The walls were white, the furniture was white, the rugs were white and so was Mae West.

She was even shorter than Eddie G. Robinson, but unlike Eddie, she was wearing a silk negligee. That struck me as odd, as did her crew of servants. There were four or five of them. They were all young, male, and muscular. I felt as if I had stepped into the middle of one of her Las Vegas revues.

Nothing too memorable was said by either of us, although she did let me know that the feelings were mutual, that she thought Fields was over-rated as a funny man and a pain in the neck to work with because of his constant boozing.

I shared with her the information that both I and Carlotta Monti agreed that Fields wasn't very funny, and that a good deal of his lasting popularity was because it was so easy for people to imitate his nasal delivery. It stood to reason that if they thought their version of "my little chickadee" or "my little kumquat" was hilarious, so was his.

Ms. West agreed that Fields had never written a funny line and, what's more, there was nothing funny about being a drunk.

The interview didn't take too long. For one thing, I was smoking three packs-a-day at the time and was dying for a cigarette. For another, I felt she wanted me gone. After all, I not only didn't have bulging biceps, but I definitely clashed with the decor.

***

Because I was such a fan of Jack Benny, I should have been even more nervous about meeting him than I was. At the time, he had probably made me laugh more than any other person in the world. I had been listening to his radio show for years even before he made his successful transition to TV.

I knew all his sidekicks, including Don Wilson, Dennis Day, Eddie "Rochester" Anderson, Mary Livingston -- Mrs. Benny in real life --

Phil Harris, Mel Blanc, Frank Nelson, Sheldon Leonard, and Artie Auerbach, who played the Jewish-accented Mr. Kitzel.

Besides his regular sitcom, Benny had brought off one of the most hilarious bits I had ever seen on one of his comedy specials. Playing off his persona as a terrible violinist, soloist Benny took the stage dressed in tails, carrying his violin. Behind him, three of the Marquis Chimps, also dressed in formal attire, took their seats. They, too, carried musical instruments.

The four of them began to perform. But within a few seconds of putting up with Benny's atrocious bowing, first one chimp, then the other, took his instrument and left the stage. A disgruntled Benny looked at the third chimp, almost daring him to move. The chimp gazed back at Benny. Finally, Benny placed his chin against the violin and resumed playing. Within seconds, the third chimp had heard enough and followed the other two.

What made Benny special was that he was always the butt of the joke, whether the joke involved his musicianship, his age, or his legendary cheapness.

As I said, I would normally have been very nervous about entering his home. But by the time we met, I had been writing for the *L.A. Times* for several years. Mine was a popular column, but, in addition, I had already written about Groucho Marx, Oscar Levant, George Burns, Jack Webb, Billy Wilder, Eddie G. Robinson, and a slew of other people he knew.

But either he didn't take the Sunday *Times*, didn't read my stuff, or failed to connect me with that writer. It was perhaps the most off-putting interview I had ever conducted. It wasn't that he didn't answer my questions or gave me short shrift. It was that he felt he had to say my name every time he responded. So, he would say things like "I have the best writers in the business, Burt" or "Mary really did hate acting, but she was so good, Burt, I had to keep using her."

The problem was that he never said "Burt." He knew my name began with a "B," so he'd call me Bob, Bruce, Ben, Bill, Barry, Brian, anything but my own name. I corrected him the first few times, but after that I stopped bothering. I might have thought age was creeping up on him, but my name seemed to be the only thing he couldn't remember.

I knew he wasn't being intentionally rude because everyone I had ever spoken to who knew him assured me he was the kindest big star in the business.

Perhaps someone named Burt had frightened his mother when she was pregnant.

Or perhaps some mysteries are never supposed to be solved. That's what makes them mysteries.

***

I rarely had any direct dealings with politicians, at least not too many after my UCLA friends Howard Berman and Henry Waxman were elected to Congress and sailed off to Washington, D.C.

But in 1972, I decided I wanted to get inside the head of someone who actually believed that in a nation of nearly 300 million he was the best person to be elected president. I couldn't even imagine how someone with that huge an ego could even carry it around. I would have thought it required several strong men to cart it from room to room.

I decided I would contact Hubert Humphrey, who was, as I recall, leading in the polls in January. I never heard back from his people, though, so I tried to contact the one contender for the nomination who was actually campaigning in L.A. And even though at the time he only was at 3% in the polls, I decided that George McGovern would meet my needs.

I wound up spending an entire day with him as he went from one venue to another, delivering the same boring talking points in the same boring way.

In private, as we were driven from one place to another, he was as boring and as arrogant about his beliefs and as humorless as he was on the stump. Nobody could have been as surprised as I was when he wound up being nominated that summer.

He had been so totally unimpressive that for the first time in my life, I seriously considered sitting out a presidential election. I simply couldn't see voting for him or providing Richard Nixon with a second term.

It just so happened that my then-wife and I were expecting our first child in August. My favorite name has always been "Max," but she didn't care for it. As a negotiating ploy, knowing she was a fan of McGovern, I said I was planning to vote for Nixon. She begged me not to cancel out her vote. I said I would vote for McGovern if she would acquiesce on the kid's name.

I could have cheated once I was in the voting booth, but she had gone along with naming the baby in August, so I voted for McGovern in November. Fortunately, hardly anyone else did. I wound up with a Max and McGovern wound up with a shellacking, carrying only Minnesota.

***

Until I joined the writing staff for *Diagnosis Murder*, I had never had a staff job. I had always preferred the freedom and variety of writing freelance. But necessity is the mother of selling out, and so I found myself working on a medical mystery series.

Never having worked on a staff before, I had nothing to compare it with, but my colleagues all told me I had lucked out. Between them, they had worked as writer-producers on a great many TV dramas, ranging from *Magnum, P.I.* to *Cagney & Lacey*, from *Perry Mason* to *Jake & the Fatman*, and they all agreed that working with Dick Van Dyke was as good as it got.

During the two years I served as Executive Story Consultant on the show, I found no reason to disagree. Although Dick never lunched with the writers, actors, and the crew, preferring to eat in his trailer, he never displayed a moment's worth of temperament. Whenever I had a favor to ask, whether it was to pose with me for a photo or to agree to let a friend and a brother-in-law do a walk-on, he was ever-obliging.

But it went beyond such courtesies. Our offices were on the second floor of a massive building in the San Fernando Valley that housed our interior sets on the ground floor. To get to the second floor meant going up one of those silly cement staircases, the steps of which are embedded with decorative stones. Even I, who was several years younger than Van Dyke, hated going up and down those steps. But one day, I looked up from my desk and there, standing in my open doorway, was Dick Van Dyke.

It seems he wished to change a line in the script they were currently shooting, and was seeking my permission!

Even if you forget about the hazards of that damn staircase, this was an amazing act of respect. For one thing, he was the star of the show. He did not require my permission to change a line or a hundred lines. And even if he wanted to drop a line or wished to have me re-write a line, he could have had me summoned to the soundstage. This was clearly a mensch, in a town where menschen don't grow on trees.

Van Dyke wasn't just kind to his writers. During the two seasons I was there, he had all five of his grandkids, his daughter, and his son-in-law, appear on the show. Of course his son, Barry, appeared as a co-star, and a season before I arrived, he had his brother Jerry do a guest role. Apparently, Dick subscribed to the belief that the family that plays together stays together.

In contrast, we once had a woman, Nancy Malone, direct one of my episodes. Because I'd been upstairs all day working on another script, I had not gone downstairs to see how the shoot was going.

The next morning, though, I saw the dailies. I couldn't believe what I was watching. There had been a very long scene involving a poker game. What I saw was a scene that might have been amusing in a comedy, perhaps one starring the Three Stooges, but had me in near-apoplexy.

One poker hand would end, but nobody was collecting the chips. The next dealer wasn't even bothering to collect all the cards from the previous hand, but was blithely dealing hands from a deck that might have had 25 cards in it.

I asked the producer what was going on. Not being a poker player, although I would have thought the problem was as obvious as showing a baseball game in which batters would hit the ball and then run to third base instead of first, she had failed to notice the obvious.

What I couldn't imagine was how the actors and the crew had let this happen. Only later did I learn that the director had so put off everyone with her arrogant manner that they had decided to let her sabotage herself. I might have felt the same -- and did once I actually had to deal with her -- but it was my episode and our show, and we had them re-shoot the scene correctly.

***

If you ever wonder why people become actors, the answer came to me when we were shooting a low budget feature, *Angels on Tap*, that I had written and was co-producing.

We were shooting our interiors at a Moose Lodge in El Segundo, a community south of L.A.'s international airport, a location that placed it between 25 and 80 miles from the homes of our five stars, Ed Asner, Marion Ross, Alan Rachins, Jamie Farr, and Ron Masak.

Because we couldn't start shooting until closing time and we had to be gone by the time they were ready for early arrivals in the morning, our hours ran from midnight to 8 a.m.

But our actors, whose ages ranged from 73-87 and averaged 82, were ready to hit their marks as soon as the cameras began rolling.

In a few cases, I had been able to call in favors of friends, but two of the five were people I had never even met before they showed up in El Segundo. Fortunately, they all liked the script, but you have to understand that based on what we were able to pay these Emmy winners and nominees, they probably weren't making minimum wage, especially after you deducted the price of gas.

My point is that they were showing up because they were actors,

151

and actors simply love to act. So, at an age when most people are content to stay home and play with the grandkids or watch reruns of, say, *Mary Tyler Moore*, *Happy Days*, *L.A. Law*, *M*A*S*H*, or *Murder, She Wrote*, my five troupers were working through the wee hours of the morning doing what they seemed to believe they were put on earth to do; namely, put on a show.

ALL IN HIS FAMILY

Although I had a small role in "Cold Turkey," a movie shot in Iowa by producer-director Norman Lear, we hadn't really spent much time together.

At that point, he was simply half of a successful comedy writing and producing team along with Bud Yorkin. His TV empire built upon the success of "All in the Family," "Maude," "The Jeffersons," and "Fernwood Tonight," was still a bit in the future.

But once his fame came, it was fast and furious. He was showing up on the covers of news magazines and having his opinion sought on everything from democracy to race relations, from the U.N. to the state of the American educational system.

Everything I knew about him came to me through the various news sources. That was until I was invited to take part in a TV conference in Richmond, Virginia. One night, a few of us on the panel went out for drinks. After a couple of, what I believe were mai-tai's, one of Lear's two top executives in his production company, a woman in her 40s, let her hair down.

It seems that although she had the same responsibility as her male counterpart, she had recently discovered that he was making $125,000 while she was getting paid $75,000. If that seems paltry for Hollywood executives, you have to keep in mind this was nearly 40 years ago.

Frankly, I was shocked at the revelation. I wasn't surprised that a man was being paid more than a woman for doing the exact same job, understand, but that the man writing the checks was the same fellow who had recently appeared at a NOW convention and received an ovation from the ladies when he presented the group a check for $250,000 in the name of Edith Bunker, she of "All in the Family" fame.

At the time, I thought that was one of the clearest examples I had ever encountered of Hollywood hypocrisy in action. When nobody's looking, he stiffs a female employee, but then turns around and, to a chorus of rich ladies' cheers, makes a huge donation in the name of a fictitious TV character.

The next time I saw Lear was at his home in Brentwood, where I had gone on an assignment for *Esquire*.

Being a limousine liberal, he couldn't help embarrassing himself. The first instance was when we were seated in his living room and he spotted his black maid crossing the room. I guess he figured he had to explain her presence, lest I take him for a plantation owner. I forget what her name was, but let's call her Ruth. "Ruth," he said to me, "is just like one of the family."

I admit I was slightly taken aback because I didn't know that people in real life were still spouting such inane clichés. Well, I suppose you could say Ruth was like one of the family except that she was the one paid to fetch and carry for every other member of the family. I suppose it's fair to say that Cinderella was like one of the family, too, except that, unlike Ruth, she didn't get Sundays off.

The thing is, I had no problem with Lear having a black maid. I'm sure she was being paid regularly, although probably not as much as a butler would have been paid in the Lear home, and she certainly had pleasant surroundings. But I guess in Lear's Hollywood circle, having a black servant was too much like owning a black slave.

But Norman wasn't finished flashing his liberal credentials. He told me that he was very proud of his young son. It seems the lad had been coming home from nursery school or perhaps it was kindergarten and speaking glowingly about his new friend. It was only when Norman and the third Mrs. Lear attended a PTA meeting that they discovered their son's friend was black. Norman couldn't get over the fact that although their son had mentioned the kid several times, he had never once mentioned his race.

It took me a while to figure out why that would strike Norman as such a wonderful thing. If it had been my son, I would have wondered if he was vision-impaired. I'm not suggesting there was anything wrong about little Lear having a black chum, but not to even mention that he was black strikes me as peculiar.

I mean, if Lear and his wife had shown up at the school and discovered that their son's little six-year-old buddy had a beard, would they also have popped their buttons with pride or would they have rushed him to an optometrist?

Near the end of the interview, Norman confessed that he had nearly lost his entire fortune because he had set out to create a publishing empire. He admitted that it was only through the intervention of some friends that he hadn't lost the entire $100 million he had left after divorcing Frances, his second of three wives, after 30 years of marriage.

At the door, I set our political differences aside and told him: "Norman, the next time you feel the urge to do something that stupid, give me a call and I'll talk you down. Perhaps it still hasn't occurred to you, but take my word for it that although there is precious little difference between $100 million and $200 million, there is a chasm wider than the Grand Canyon between having $100 million and being broke."

BILLY THE KIDDER

I have been blessed in my life to have known, worked with and even been friends with a large number of fascinating characters, including Groucho Marx, Oscar Levant, Jack Webb, George Kennedy, Merrill Heatter, Dick Van Dyke, William Peter Blatty, Henry Mancini, and Lizabeth Scott.

But one of the most memorable was Billy Wilder, the man who started out in Vienna earning his keep by waltzing rich old ladies around the floor at afternoon tea dances. The dancing stopped when circumstances dictated that he remain one step ahead of Hitler by moving to France and then the U.S., where he learned vernacular English by watching movies in the 1930s.

Ultimately and perhaps even inevitably, he landed in Hollywood, where he made his mark writing such classics as *Ninotchka*, *Ball of Fire*, and *Hold Back the Dawn*.

It was the last of these that led him to confront his bosses at Paramount and demand the opportunity to direct. As he tells it: "The best thing that ever happened to me was being teamed with Charles Brackett. The worst was having Mitchell Leisen direct our scripts. Every time we wanted to discuss a character or a plot point we would find him down in costuming, counting the pleats on some dress. He should have been a costume designer. Fortunately, Preston Sturges had recently gotten the opportunity to direct his own scripts, and he'd turned out one hit after another for the studio. I'm certain the bosses figured Wilder would write something artsy-fartsy, fall on his face and go back to being a nice little screenwriter."

Instead, he and Brackett wrote *The Major and the Minor* for the previous year's Oscar winner, Ginger Rogers, and it was Paramount's biggest moneymaker in 1942.

Wilder was off and running, turning out the likes of *The Lost*

157

Weekend, *Double Indemnity*, *A Foreign Affair*, *Sunset Blvd.*, *Stalag 17*, *Sabrina*, *Some Like It Hot*, and *The Apartment*.

Some were original scripts, some were adaptations, some were comedies, and others were dramas. I once asked him how he decided which to write, and he said it all depended on his mood. If he was happy, he'd work on a drama; if he was down in the dumps, he'd make a comedy.

Sometimes, nitpickers would point out that Wilder always wrote with collaborators, but I suspect that's because he was very sociable and enjoyed the company. Although he did collaborate with several others, for the most part, he wrote with two other men. The first was Brackett, who, after *Sunset Blvd.*, decided he had worked in Wilder's shadow long enough and struck out on his own. Wilder replaced him with I.A.L. ("Izzy") Diamond and went on to write two of his best, *Some Like It Hot* and *The Apartment*.

The most telling thing about Wilder as a collaborator is that, with the possible exception of Raymond Chandler, with whom he wrote *Double Indemnity* because Brackett found the material too sordid for his taste, none of them ever wrote as well alone or with others.

The one thing he brought with him from Europe, aside from a certain mix of cynicism and sentimentality, was an old world civility that required him to refer even to those he disliked as "Mr.," as in "Mr. Leisen and Mr. Raft."

I mention George Raft because when Wilder was casting *Double Indemnity*, he was able to score Barbara Stanwyck, but he couldn't get any of Paramount's leading men to accept the role of Walter Neff, the insurance agent who, in tandem with his lover, murders her husband. "Finally," as Wilder reports, "I hit bottom and gave the script to George Raft. He got back to me and said he'd do it, but he wondered at what point he'd get to flip his collar. I asked him what he meant. He said, 'You know -- where I flip the collar on my jacket and show her the badge and arrest the dame for killing her husband.' Apparently, he couldn't read any better than he could act. I explained that they both killed her husband. That's when Raft decided he wasn't interested."

Yet the movie got made with Fred MacMurray as Neff. "How," I asked Wilder, "had that come about?"

"When Mr. MacMurray initially turned me down, he said that he wasn't up to such a dramatic role. He said, 'I'm just an ex-saxophone player.' After being turned down by Raft, I went back and told him that an ex-saxophone player was exactly what I was looking for in the part."

It reminded me that I always thought that MacMurray's two best roles were both with Wilder, the other one being the lecherous boss in *The Apartment*.

"And I had to fight him that time, too. He read the script and liked it, but said it would ruin his image because by that time he was doing the TV series with the little boys and making movies for Disney. I pointed out that *Double Indemnity* had damaged his image so badly that he wound up being the highest-paid actor on the Paramount lot."

Speaking of casting reminded me that I thought the two worst-cast actors in his movies had been Humphrey Bogart in *Sabrina* and Gary Cooper in *Love in the Afternoon*. Oddly enough, he agreed with me. "I wanted Mr. Cary Grant both times, but I could never get him. I don't know why. Maybe my German accent frightened him. The bad thing about *Sabrina* was that Mr. Bogart got wind of the fact he hadn't been my first choice. He took it very personally and behaved very badly on the set. Because he knew he couldn't take his resentment out on me, he would insult the other writer, young Ernest Lehman. One day he was being particularly obnoxious and I announced on the set that shooting would stop for the day and not resume until Mr. Bogart publicly apologized to Mr. Lehman. The next day, he did so. But it was not a happy experience."

Although for 25 years, I don't think anyone anywhere ever had a hand in making such a dazzling array of movies, there came a time when for whatever reason the magic disappeared. For me, it happened after he won Oscars for writing, directing and producing *The Apartment*. Although his biggest grosser came next with *Irma la Douce*, which re-teamed Jack Lemmon and Shirley MacLaine, I thought it was awful, and things didn't improve with the likes of *Front Page*, *Avanti!*, *Buddy, Buddy*, *The Private Life of Sherlock Holmes*, *Fedora*, and the loathsome *Kiss Me, Stupid*.

By the time we met, between his advanced age and his string of flops, Wilder wasn't even able to pitch projects to the studios. Mainly, he worked on creating art in a box, but he kept jotting down ideas for movies and sticking them in a drawer. He confessed that the notion behind *The Apartment* started out with 13 words on a little piece of paper: "Who was the guy who let them use his apartment in *Brief Encounter?*"

For those unfamiliar with Noel Coward's bittersweet 1945 romance, which starred Trevor Howard and Celia Johnson, it involves two married people who fall in love and use his friend's place for their assignations. Perhaps because the friend is never seen, Wilder couldn't stop wondering who he was. It took 15 years but he finally showed up as an overly-ambitious company man named C.C. Baxter.

Back in the days of the blacklist, the writers and directors who had been called to testify before a congressional committee were called "The Hollywood 10," but after they pled the 5th, refusing to answer whether they were or ever had been members of the Communist Party, they were referred to as "The Unfriendly 10." At lunch one day, I asked Wilder if he had actually quipped, "Two of them had talent, the other eight were just unfriendly." He admitted he had, but said he shouldn't have because, although it was true, it was unkind.

Although I had the opportunity to rave about *Some Like It Hot* and *The Apartment,* most of my career as a movie critic coincided with Wilder's fallow period. And as I later discovered, he was well aware that I'd been panning his movies one after another. Which is the reason I was so moved when after I'd known him for a while, he inscribed a photo: "To Burt Prelutsky, one of the few journalists I both like and respect. Billy Wilder, '95."

It's just one of the reasons that even though he always insisted I call him Billy, I always thought of him as Mr. Wilder.

MY FRIEND,
THE ODD-LOOKING GUY

There are certain people that one meets and befriends, and when you stop and think about it, you are amazed that such a thing had come to pass.

One of those people was Norman Lloyd. Until I met him playing tennis at the home and on the court that Sam Goldwyn, Jr. had inherited from his father, I knew him only as the somewhat spooky-looking actor who had fallen to his death from the Statue of Liberty in Hitchcock's wartime thriller, *Saboteur*, and as the sardonic Private Archimbeau in *A Walk in the Sun*, who didn't have time to worry about his fate in World War II because he was already fixated on the next war, which he was certain would take place in Tibet.

He was also sardonic in real life, but very kind and fascinating. After all, it's not every day that you run into someone who not only played tennis with the likes of Douglas Fairbanks and Charlie Chaplin on Chaplin's own court, but who wound up working with Hitchcock, not only as an actor, but as the co-producer of Hitchcock's TV show.

He also found time to be a member of Orson Welles' Mercury Theatre. When Welles brought his company to Hollywood to make a movie, Lloyd tagged along. But when RKO nixed his first project, Welles begged everyone to stick around even though they were now off salary. He had another idea for a movie.

Although Norman's instinct was to stick it out, when he received a call from fellow Mercury player Everett Sloane saying he needed to make a living and was headed back to New York, Norman and his wife Peggy decided to follow suit.

As it happened, Sloane didn't pack up and leave. Instead, he stuck around and got to appear in *Citizen Kane*, in a role that he would have had to compete with Lloyd to play, that of Kane's long-time associate, Bernstein. However, it wasn't a total loss for Lloyd because when Alfred Hitchcock asked Welles' own associate, John Houseman, if he knew anyone who could play the assassin in *Saboteur*, Houseman recommended him. And so began Lloyd's very long association and friendship with Hitchcock.

Lloyd even got to join Buster Keaton in Chaplin's *Limelight*, which, he claimed, was intended as a cinematic love letter from Chaplin to his wife, Oona, mother to eight of his children. According to Norman, Claire Bloom got the role of the old vaudevillian's love object because she so closely resembled Chaplin's beloved Oona.

One day when Norman and I were sharing confessions, he mentioned that his greatest regret was that when Hitchcock was reaching the end of his life, Hitch, as Norman always referred to him, had asked Norman to work with him on a movie project that Norman knew would never come to fruition. And, so, Norman turned him down. It still caused him pain years after Hitchcock's death. "I owed the man so much. It would only have cost me a little bit of time to help re-pay the enormous debt."

There have been a number of amazingly long marriages in Hollywood, a town where after five years of wedlock people are accustomed to shake their heads in awe and say, "I never thought it would last this long."

Among the longest unions were Bob Hope's, who lasted 69 years, mainly because Mrs. Hope was a Catholic who didn't believe in divorce and because she was therefore willing to stay home and raise the kids while he cavorted around the world until he was finally too old to cavort; and Karl Malden's, who made it to 70 years before he died. But the champs were Norman and Peggy Lloyd, who combined love, marrying young, and good genes, to make it all the way to 75 years before her passing in 2011 at the age of 98.

Norman has already made it to 102 and even being hit by a car a few years ago has only impinged on his tennis, not his longevity.

A M*A*S*H NOTE
FOR LARRY GELBART

It was over 30 years ago that I first laid eyes on the remarkable comedy writer Larry Gelbart. The occasion was our high school's 50th anniversary. I had been selected to host the celebration in the auditorium. It was also my duty to reminisce about Fairfax High School during the time I was there in the 1950s. It was Gelbart's job to report on the 1940s. As I recall, movie producer Mike Frankovich handled the 1930s and band singer Martha Tilton recalled the 1920s.

It so happened that Ms. Tilton had left before graduating because she'd been hired to go off with some band and begin her singing career, so it was also to be the occasion of my presenting her with her long-overdue diploma. As I handed it to her, I remarked that she would now be able to get a job at the post office.

Although I got to introduce Gelbart to the audience, we didn't actually meet.

Several months later, in a weekly column I was still writing for the *L.A. Times*, I took exception to the constant trashing of TV. For all its obvious faults, I pointed out that over the years TV, not Broadway, books, or the movies, was the place to find the best comedy in America. I went on to mention ten or twelve of the anonymous men and women most responsible for writing the funniest material. Naturally, Larry Gelbart, as one of the stalwarts of Sid Caesar's *Show of Shows*, was one of the names on my list.

The next day, I received a phone call. It was Larry and he started out by apologizing. He said that he and his wife, Pat, had dreaded going to the Fairfax High bash, but that I had been very funny and they had had a terrific time. It seems he had meant to call me, but it had slipped his mind. Now he was calling to thank me for the mention in the column.

Oddly enough, I was anxious to get off the phone. Although I appreciate compliments as much as the next guy, assuming the next guy likes compliments, I'm the guy who prefers them in writing. Even when I receive them over the phone, I feel like I'm blushing and have lost the power of speech.

After being praised, just saying "Thank you" seems terribly lame, whereas returning the compliment, no matter how sincerely, seems awfully phony. But just before I was able to mumble my thanks and hang up, I heard him say, "I understand you sometimes write for TV. If you ever come up with an idea for a *M*A*S*H* script, just shoot it over to me. I'm here at 20th Century-Fox."

It had long been my wish to write comedy for TV, but aside from managing to accrue some credits on *Dragnet* and *McMillan & Wife*, the only sitcom I'd written for was a single episode of *The Governor & J.J.*, a short-lived failure.

So, while I was greatly motivated, my problem was that I wasn't a fan of the show. I hadn't liked the movie and the only time I'd watched an episode, it just seemed like all those other lousy service comedies, like *Don't Go Near the Water* and *Operation Petticoat*, that I had already come to loathe.

The part of the story that even I have a hard time believing is that an hour earlier, I had been in the office of the agency that represented me. It had been a two-person agency, but that morning the female partner had called to suggest I come in and meet their new associate. I was told he was going to rep the comedy writers.

Naturally, I immediately drove over, anxious to meet the person who was going to show me the way to the Promised Land. At the time, the agency had three treatments I had written for TV series -- one was a comedy western, one was a proposal for a private eye series, and the third was a family sitcom.

The guy started out by telling me what was wrong with all three. But he was such a schmuck, he kept mixing up characters from one show with the others. When he finished demolishing my work, he announced he had a terrific idea for a series that he thought I should write up. When I asked him why he would want me to write it inasmuch as he hated my work, he explained that this time he would be around to help me. Great, I remember thinking, I've now got an agent who wants to break into the business. I told him I'd think about it.

He seemed somewhat disgruntled, but invited me to tell him which series I would like to write for. I rattled off *Mary Tyler Moore*, *Bob Newhart*, *All in the Family*, and would have continued, but he had suddenly leaned forward and was holding his head between his hands. I thought he had suddenly developed a migraine and asked him what the matter was. He looked up and said, "You're only naming the hottest shows on the air." No migraine, it was just me.

"Okay," I suggested, "I have a family to support, so how about my agreeing to write for any show you can line up."

"Well, at least that's a possibility." But it was obvious that he considered even that modest request highly improbable.

So when I hung up the phone on Gelbart, the first thing I did was call my new agent and tell him that apparently the hottest shows on the air weren't locked up quite as much as he thought, and that he was fired.

For about two seconds, I felt great. Then it hit me that I was not only unemployed, but that I no longer had an agent. Talk about your pyrrhic victories!

Desperate for an idea, I sat down with my steno pad and prayed for a miracle. The miracle came in the form of an idea about an injured soldier showing up at the 4077th, claiming to be Jesus Christ.

"Quo Vadis, Captain Chandler?" led to seven additional *M*A*S*H* scripts, a shot at several other sitcoms, a nomination for a Humanitas Award, and ultimately swung open the doors to writing TV movies.

Because I owed Gelbart a debt that I could never hope to repay, I was grateful when he called one day and asked me for a favor. It seems the Writer's Guild was hosting a tribute to Larry that very evening, and Mel Shavelson, who was scheduled to emcee the event, had taken ill. Larry wondered if I would fill in.

Inasmuch as my responsibilities would be pretty much limited to pointing to people in the audience during the Q&A session, and in some cases repeating their questions into a microphone, I felt I was up to the task, if just barely.

Larry was his usual droll and hilarious self. The most memorable moment, though, came during the intermission when Larry and I left the stage to sit with his wife in the front row.

A young fellow came down the aisle and knelt down next to Larry. As expected, he began by saying what a great fan he was and how, being a writer himself, he regarded Gelbart as a role model.

Larry, being far more adept at handling compliments than I because, no doubt, he had had so much more experience receiving them, was smiling and nodding graciously. The big surprise came when the young fan concluded his remarks by saying, "And that's why I'm so excited to be re-writing *Rough Cut*."

Rough Cut, you see, was a script Gelbart had been writing for Burt Reynolds and David Niven. Until that moment, Gelbart hadn't know that he'd been replaced by the back-stabbing producer.

So, forget all the stuff he wrote for the movies (*Tootsie, Oh, God! The Wrong Box*); the stage (*A Funny Thing Happened on the Way to the Forum, Mastergate, City of Angels*); and TV (Sid Caesar, *Weapons of Mass Distraction, Barbarians at the Gate*).

Forget that at the tender age of 16, while attending Fairfax High, Gelbart would go, still wearing his ROTC uniform, to join a bunch of middle-aged men to write *Duffy's Tavern* and a little later, Bob Hope's radio show. After all, anyone with the appropriate amount of God-given talent, wit, and staying power, could do the very same thing for 60-odd years.

But the fact that he could sit quietly and listen to this pisher break the news that he had replaced Gelbart on a writing project and keep on smiling, shake his hand and wish him luck, tells you all you need to know about what sort of mensch Larry Gelbart was.

WORDS & MUSIC

Recently, a friend, knowing of my high regard for motion picture scores asked me about my favorites. One thing led to another and I began sharing anecdotes about some of America's great composers and lyricists, more than a few of which had been related to me by the men themselves and some of which I had merely read about. They struck me as worth sharing.

There is a reason I have always wished I had had a musical education and could have been a composer. For one thing, nobody needs to translate your work to be appreciated in foreign countries. For another, if you're lucky enough or talented enough, the music just seems to flow out like spring water.

For instance, I once heard about an occasion when Oscar Hammerstein wrote the lyrics to a song before Richard Rodgers had started work on the tune. Hammerstein left his partner's New York apartment and took a taxi to his own. By the time he opened the door, his phone was ringing. It was Rodgers playing the song on his piano.

Another time, it involved the team of Harold Arlen and Ted Koehler. They, too, had apartments in New York City. Each morning, lyricist Koehler would walk over to Arlen's place, and together they would walk to their office. But this one morning, it was extremely cold and blustery, so Koehler suggested they take a cab. But Arlen was in the mood for walking, so while swinging his arms for warmth, he started marching up the street and humming to his own beat. The music he was humming turned out to be "I Love a Parade" by the time they reached their office and Koehler put words to it.

I once had occasion to interview Henry Mancini, the man who with collaborator Johnny Mercer created history when they won back-to-back Best Song Oscars with "The Days of Wine and Roses" and "Moon River." I asked him the same question I invariably ask every composer: How do you know when you write a song that someone else didn't write it first? I mean, you start out with a few notes and one thing leads to another and, voila! you have a song with your name on it. But how can you be sure it's not something your mother sang to you when you were an infant?

Whenever I ask that question, I always worry that the reaction will be, "That's the dumbest thing I've ever heard." But Mancini assured me he worried about that very thing every time he composed a tune. He did go on to say that his wife Ginny had been a band singer, and if he played the song and it didn't ring a bell with either of them, he felt he was on pretty safe ground.

It was the same question I put to Michel Legrand, who was visiting from his home in France. He started off saying that he didn't concern himself with such things, but then paused and said, "Well, there was this one time."

Legrand, whose work was pretty much reserved to writing film scores for the likes of *Brian's Song* and *The Umbrellas of Cherbourg*, also wrote songs for movies, including "I Will Wait for You," "The Windmills of Your Mind" and the entire score of *Yentl*. But, once, as he recalled, he had a piece of music in his head that wouldn't leave him in peace until he put it to paper.

He then proceeded to invite all of his friends to his Paris studio so he could play it for them. They were all very impressed, but the next day, one of them called Legrand and said he thought it had sounded familiar. It seems that Legrand had been the second person, the first being Pierre De Geyter in the 19th century, to compose "The Internationale," the anthem of the Communist Party!

Not having a musical background, another question that kept recurring is whether classical musicians can really tell the difference between one pianist and another, assuming they're both good enough to perform as soloists. Could a trained musician really tell, sight unseen, if he was listening to Arthur Rubenstein, Van Cliburn, or Vladimir Horowitz?

When I met Itzhak Perlman, the Israeli violinist who, as a result of a childhood bout with polio, performs sitting on a chair, I put the question to him. He said that he generally can, but admitted that he was once riding in a car and heard a violinist on the radio. He could tell the guy was good, but he couldn't come up with a name until the piece ended and the announcer identified the artist as.... Itzhak Perlman!

When I interviewed Sammy Cahn, the four-time Oscar winning lyricist, I asked him if he had ever considered writing the music as well as the words. He said the die had been cast when he was still a child and his family moved from one cold water flat in New York to another. When they got to the new place, they discovered that the former tenant had left behind a piano and a violin. When Mrs. Cahn saw the musical instruments, she pointed at Sammy's sister and said, "Piano;" then at Sammy, "Violin." He said that if she had reversed her decision, he'd have been able to play the piano well enough to compose at it.

Cahn also told me why he liked Prince Charles so much. It seems that the Reagans once invited several musicians to perform at the White House in the Prince's honor. They invited Sammy, but only as a guest. And anyone who knew him knew that singing his own songs was what he loved most in life. Although he didn't sing all that well, he had a load of panache and had not only recorded an album of Sammy singing Sammy, he had performed in concert in New York.

At the White House gala, Sammy was seated right behind his old pal President Reagan. Knowing that Reagan wasn't one for late hours, Sammy saw his opportunity ticking away by the second. Suddenly, just as Reagan appeared ready to call it a night, the Prince who was seated next to him, said, "I noticed that Mr. Cahn is here this evening, and I was wondering if you could possibly persuade him to sing for us."

Knowing Sammy Cahn, he was probably out of his chair before Reagan even had time to think about it.

Some years later, Cahn was in London at one of those royal command performances where all the celebrities stand in line in the theatre foyer waiting for some member of the Royal Family to pass by and say a few cordial words.

This evening it was Prince Charles and Lady Di. As soon as Charles spotted Cahn, he leaned over and began whispering in his wife's ear, no doubt informing her that Cahn had written nearly one hundred of the songs Frank Sinatra had recorded, about three times as many as the person in second place.

But Fate will have its little jokes, so naturally when the royals reached Sammy, Lady Di stuck out her hand and said, "I'm very pleased to meet you, Mr. Cahn. I just love 'I Did It My Way.'" Close, as they say, but no cigar. That one just happened to have been written for Sinatra by Paul Anka.

When I interviewed David Raksin, who wrote memorable scores for *The Bad and the Beautiful* and *Forever Amber*, I was shocked to learn that even though his Hollywood career stretched from 1936, when he helped arrange Charley Chaplin's score for *Modern Times*, to his 1983 dramatic score for *The Day After*, he had only been nominated once for an Academy Award, whereas many of his less-talented colleagues had had to add rooms to their home in order to accommodate their Oscars.

His best shot at an Oscar came in 1944 when he composed the haunting score for *Laura*. Unfortunately, in those days, a studio could only submit one score for consideration and because studio boss Daryl Zanuck had personally produced *Wilson*, a cinematic ode to his favorite president, Zanuck opted to go with Alfred Newman's rather pedestrian score for *Wilson*.

The story Raksin told me about how his *Laura* score came to be sounded like a corny 20th Century-Fox concoction. He claimed that he had already submitted music to producer-director Otto Preminger, but Preminger had been disappointed and decided to use the Duke Ellington composition, "Sophisticated Lady." But Raksin begged him to hold off until after the weekend.

When Raksin arrived home that Friday evening, he found a letter from his wife, who was vacationing in New York. She let him know she was getting a divorce. According to Raksin, he placed the "Dear David" letter on his music stand and used it as his muse. Monday morning, he delivered the score to Preminger.

At the time, I must confess it sounded a little too Hollywood to be true, but then I realized that even in Hollywood, guys don't often boast about being dumped by their wives.

Next we come to the remarkable Johnny Mercer, one of the three or four greatest lyricists who ever lived, a singer, a sometime composer, and one of the co-founders of Capitol Records. He was also the fellow who wound up writing the lyrics to "Laura."

In some ways, Mercer was a model citizen. For instance, when his gambler father died, leaving a pile of debts in his hometown of Savannah, Georgia, Johnny paid off every last one of them.

However, Mercer drank far too much far too often, and when he'd get in his cups, he would insult everyone in the vicinity. The next day, he would send a dozen roses to those he'd hurt.

Once, when I was interviewing singer Jo Stafford, I asked her if she had ever met Mercer. She had. She liked him and naturally admired his talent. But one night when they were having dinner in a restaurant, he started drinking. She stood up and when he asked where she was going, she said, "Home. I don't want you sending me any roses in the morning."

It almost sounds like a Mercer lyric.

Finally, I was good friends with Harry Ruby, the fellow who wrote such hits as "Three Little Words," "Who's Sorry Now?" and "A Kiss to Build a Dream On," as well as a few of the tunes made famous by Groucho Marx, such as "Hail, Hail, Fredonia" and "I'm Against It."

In fact, he once told me that the perfect marriage would unite him and Groucho in holy matrimony because they were two elderly men of means who both loved baseball. In fact, he loved it so much that he never forgave Jack Norworth for writing "Take Me Out to the Ballgame." As he put it, "I should have written it. That son of a bitch didn't even like baseball!"

And once when I asked him what he imagined Heaven was like, Harry said, "It's where someone has to pay you a nickel every time you catch them whistling one of your songs."

STEPHEN J. CANNELL, A TRIBUTE

Stephen J. Cannell is my hero. But it's not because he has produced more than 1,500 hours of quality television, written over 450 episodes, and created more than 40 shows, including *The Rockford Files, The A-Team, Hunter, Riptide, 21 Jump Street, Wiseguy, The Commish, Renegade,* and *Silk Stalkings.* Heck, any 10 or 12 guys working day and night could probably have done the same.

He's surely not my hero because, at an age when most TV writers start bitching about ageism, he managed to change careers and become a best-selling novelist.

He's also not my hero because, unlike most normal writers who can't balance a checkbook or even figure out the appropriate tip on a $13 lunch, Cannell is a savvy business tycoon who not only oversaw a billion-dollar studio, but continues to own the worldwide distribution rights to over a thousand hours of Cannell-produced series and TV movies.

He's certainly not my hero because in a town in which the most popular reality show is "Switching Spouses," he and Marcia have been married for roughly a kazillion years.

It goes without saying that he's not my hero because he's won a trophy room full of Emmys and WGA awards in spite of having dyslexia. After all, it's not like he's the first person who's ever suffered from an eating disorder.

He's surely not my hero because he's tall, tan, and looks the way movie stars used to look. And you better believe it's not because Steve Cannell has more hair on his head than my dog has on its entire body.

No, Stephen J. Cannell is my hero because.... well, let's begin more or less at the beginning. Let's go back to 1988, the year of the Writer Guild's last strike. There were those in the Guild who thought the strike was a bad idea. I wasn't one of them; Cannell was.

After a meeting held by those of the loyal opposition, Cannell was widely quoted in the media. So was I. It was my honest opinion that while such people as Cannell and Steve Bochco were entitled to their opinion, inasmuch as most of their money came from producing and owning shows, they did not share the same concerns the rest of us did.

One night, my phone rang. It was Cannell calling, and he was very upset. He insisted that he was, first and foremost, a writer, and he resented what I had said.

I pointed out that I was a fan of his work and intended no insult, but there was simply no way on earth that a guy with half a dozen shows on the air could possibly be as concerned about foreign residuals and our health plan as the majority of his fellow Guild members were.

For a moment after I spoke, there was nothing but silence. I assumed he had hung up on me. Then he said, "You're right." I was so surprised, I actually said, "I am?"

But even the fact that Steve Cannell is probably the only person I have ever convinced of anything isn't the reason he's my hero.

For that, we have to jump ten years to 1998. By that time, ageism had hit me so hard that my wife and I had to sell our condo and declare bankruptcy. The only job I was able to get was as a freelancer writing celebrity profiles for Emmy magazine. When I got the assignment to write about David Chase, who had taken TV by storm by creating and producing *The Sopranos*, I naturally called Cannell, the man who'd been Chase's mentor and boss years earlier on *The Rockford Files*.

Cannell supplied me with several quotable anecdotes about the young Chase. He then asked me what I was doing these days. I said, "I'm doing this -- the occasional piece for Emmy." There was another of those long pauses. Then he said, "You're too good a writer not to be working steady."

It had been several years since anyone but my wife had spoken such words to me.

Now to put this in proper context, you have to understand that Cannell and I had never really worked together. Once, I was supposed to write an episode of *Rockford*, but a young, over-eager, overly-greedy agent cost me the opportunity. Suddenly, I'm hearing him say, "I'm taking my family to Hawaii tomorrow, but I'll call when I return and we'll have lunch."

Frankly, I didn't expect to hear from him again. But, true to his word, he called back and we got together. By this time, he had already turned his back on TV and had become a novelist. But after I told him about my bleak eight years in Hollywood's equivalent of Siberia, he said he knew a lot of people who were running shows. He said he'd look through his Rolodex when he got back to his office.

The next day, he phoned. He began by saying he didn't know anyone at any of the sitcoms, and added that most of the producers he did know seemed to be working on cable sci-fi shows. However, he thought he might have an in for me at the Dick Van Dyke medical-mystery show, *Diagnosis Murder*. He promised to check it out.

When I didn't hear anything for several days, I reverted to my usual skepticism where big, good-looking, multi-millionaires are concerned. But, then, one day, the phone rang and it was Cannell. "I didn't want you to think you'd fallen between the cracks. I have a call to Chris Abbott over at *Diagnosis Murder*, but she's still out of town and won't be back until next week. I just wanted you to know that I hadn't forgotten about you."

The thoughtfulness of that phone call, even now, all these years later, is enough to make me cry. Now you know why the man's my hero.

The next time I heard from him, it was to tell me that Abbott had returned and that she was expecting my call.

The call led to a two-year gig as the executive story consultant on the series and brought me back from the brink of suicide.

In conclusion, I would just like to say that Stephen J. Cannell is more than the sum of his hyphens, writer-producer, husband-father.

He is also the finest guardian angel since Clarence got his wings.

On September 30, 2010, at the age of 69, Steve Cannell died and got his wings for real.

RIP, GEORGE

George Kennedy died recently. It ended a friendship that had lasted nearly half a century.

I first heard from Kennedy in 1967 when, in my role as movie critic for *Los Angeles* magazine, I predicted he would win an Oscar for his performance as Dragline in *Cool Hand Luke*. He wrote me a thank-you letter. I, in turn, invited him to my housewarming.

Much to my surprise, he showed up with his wife, but stayed only briefly because they had already committed to another party. As a housewarming gift, he brought me the LP of Lalo Shiffrin's score for *Luke*.

When he happened to mention at the door that he didn't expect to win the Best Supporting Actor Oscar, I made him a $10 bet, based on my belief that Gene Hackman and Michael J. Pollard, both of whom had been nominated for *Bonnie and Clyde*, would split the vote.

I guess nobody in the history of the world has ever been happier to lose a bet than George.

He called to suggest he pay up over lunch. As Bogart put it to Claude Rains, it was the start of a beautiful friendship. Once, he even went so far as to tell me that I should never hesitate to pan one of his performances, that it wouldn't affect our relationship. As it turned out, I panned a lot of his movies, but I never thought George gave a bad performance. He always seemed perfectly natural on screen, no matter if he was playing a cop, a priest, a judge, a gunfighter, or a soldier. He didn't have a hammy bone in his entire huge body.

If he seemed to be an especially convincing member of the military, perhaps it's because he spent 16 years in the Army, some of that time trying to survive the Battle of the Bulge.

He had intended to put in a full 20 years, but his back began to act up. At the time, he had been assigned to be, of all things, the technical advisor on the old Phil Silvers sitcom, *Sgt. Bilko*. But his back got so bad and his limp became so pronounced that George decided he needed to have an operation.

However, when he visited the Army hospital, he ran into two soldiers he knew who told him that they had had the operation performed and they were in worse shape than ever.

At that point, George called off the operation and paid a visit to the producer of *Bilko*, Nat Hiken, to ask if he could keep the job even if he was no longer in the service. Hiken told him the job was his, and Kennedy retired from the Army.

After a while, Hiken began sticking Kennedy in the back row of the soldiers in the barracks Bilko would address in every episode. That led to two life-changing events. The first was that Hiken's secretary noticed Kennedy limping around the office and advised him to see her uncle, a chiropractor in the Bronx. He did, and his limp disappeared. (However, once he began appearing in Hollywood westerns, he had to visit chiropractors on a regular basis. And so, I suspect, did the horses that had to cart the three hundred pounder around.)

The other thing that happened was that Kennedy's brief appearances on a hit comedy got him an agent. The agent advised George to go to Hollywood. At the time, there were a great many western series on TV, and a lot of the heroes were very large men. Guys like Jim Arness and Clint Walker needed large villains to beat up, lest they came off looking like bullies.

Kennedy later boasted that just about every good guy on TV had at some time or another knocked him down or shot him dead.

George first became known to movie audiences when he became the villain with the hook stalking Audrey Hepburn in *Charade*. It was his sympathetic portrayal in *Luke* that saved him from being typecast as a brute and helped extend his acting career to as recently as 2014.

Because George gushed about so many of his fellow actors, but especially his fellow WWII veteran, Jimmy Stewart, that I once asked him if he had ever worked with an actor he didn't like. Reluctantly, he admitted there had been two.

The first was John Gielgud. Kennedy said that hardly a day went by on the set of the 1973 remake of *Lost Horizon* that Gielgud wouldn't mention that he was accustomed to doing Shakespeare and that he had only stooped to doing this piece of shit for the money.

While it's true that the movie was a turkey, the cast included the likes of Peter Finch, Liv Ullmann, Michael York, Sally Kellerman, and Charles Boyer. But, as Kennedy said, none of them felt the need to carry on as if they were slumming, even though they had earned their own stripes by doing the likes of *A Nun's Story*, *Cries & Whispers*, *Cabaret*, *M*A*S*H*, and *Gaslight*.

As George said, "If you're a professional and take their money, you shut up and do the best you can."

The other actor Kennedy had no use for was O.J. Simpson. It seems that every morning Simpson would bring his newspaper on the set of *Naked Gun*. But when he was finished reading it, to make certain nobody else would get his mitts on it, he'd ball it up and shove it to the bottom of a trash can. If you think about it, that sort of selfish attitude would go a long way towards explaining why the schmuck would have killed his ex-wife and her boyfriend.

Although Kennedy didn't personally dislike Paul Newman, he knew that Newman resented the fact that George had won the Oscar for *Luke*, while he had only been nominated.

Kennedy also discovered that when it was time to cast *Sometimes a Great Notion*, and the producer wanted to cast George as Newman's brother, Newman nixed it. The producer later let George know the reason was that Newman, who was 5-foot-9 hadn't been comfortable acting next to Kennedy's 6-foot-4. Instead, the Oscar-nominated role went to 5-foot-7-inch Richard Jaeckel.

In hindsight, it's probably lucky that Robert Redford was only 5-foot-10 on his tiptoes or *The Sting* and *Butch Cassidy* might never have been made.

For years, George and I would meet regularly for lunch at Art's, George's favorite deli in the San Fernando Valley. One mystery I could never solve was how he could resist the tempting aromas of corned beef and pastrami, but I never knew him to order anything but an egg salad sandwich on rye bread.

Unfortunately, once George moved to Idaho so his second wife could be close to her family, I never got to see him again. But we did exchange email and birthday greetings.

Along the way, George got into the habit of signing off as one of his favorite old-time character actors. So one time it would be Adolph Menjou, another time Beulah Bondi or Eric Blore. I then began doing the same, keeping alive the memory of all those people who helped make the movies of the 30s and 40s so memorable.

So, good night, George. Please give my regards to Charles Bickford, Fay Bainter, Peter Lorre, Charles Coburn, Edward Everett Horton, Helen Broderick, Edmund Gwenn, William Demarest, Eric Rhodes, Eve Arden, Sydney Greenstreet, Frank Morgan, Edward Arnold, Una Merkel, Harry Davenport, Richard Haydn, Oscar Homolka, Henry Travers, Eugene Palette, Margaret Hamilton, Franklin Pangborn, and the rest of the old gang.

I'm sure they've already welcomed you with open arms and an egg salad sandwich.

INDEX

CPSIA information can be obtained
at www.ICGtesting.com
Printed in the USA
FSHW020049250121
77943FS